PRAISE FOR GLENN BILL

"Glenn has been a student of my training for over 20 years. His dedication to professionalism is admirable. He lives what he works. I recommend that you give serious consideration to engaging him to create positive momentum for your company or team."

—Tom Hopkins,
Author of The National Bestseller,
How to Master the Art of Selling

"Glenn brings the fundamentals of the past into the present and future of real estate sales. He is simply the real deal!"

—Glenn Sanford,
CEO eXp World Holdings, Inc./CEO SUCCESS Enterprises

"I have spent the past 40 years dedicated to improving the business and life of 1.6 million REALTORS®. Glenn's passion and commitment to this industry is shared and his SOS Program provides the key answers and strategies that every agent is looking for!"

—Don Hobbs;
Founding Partner: International Association of Expert Partners, Ambassador & Former President of SUCCESS Enterprises/SUCCESS Magazine

"When I think about Glenn, I think about his gift, his personality, his charisma, and most of all, his caring. Glenn is the man!"

—Les Brown,
World's Leading Motivational Speaker

"When I am searching for motivating and inspiring leadership, I call Glenn. His lessons always create big impact for our community of over 50,000 mortgage lenders."

—Dave Savage,
CEO, Mortgage Coach

"Glenn's enthusiasm, energy, and delivery was just what my company needed at our kickoff event. His ideas were original and his ability to get my agents to think differently was eye-opening and motivational."

—James Bradley,
Broker/Owner at CENTURY 21 BRADLEY

"Engage with Glenn. He delivers high-energy with a side of humor, and he is passionate about it. My personal advice, don't just hire Glenn, get to know him and his story...great guy!"

—Jeffrey Gitomer,
Hall of Fame Speaker, Sales Trainer,
and New York Times Bestselling Author

"Glenn Bill is in the top .0002% of business leaders in North America today...you can trust that he stands ready to deliver excellence and exceed your expectations."

—Darren Hardy,
New York Times Bestselling Author of *The Compound Effect*,
Publisher of *Success Magazine*

"Glenn helped me understand that 'we are all in this together...buyers, sellers, agents, brokers and YOU!'"

—Libby Somerville,
Re/Max Hall of Fame, Compass Broker, Founding Member

"Glenn spoke on the big stage at our Annual Summit! He delivered passion, creativity, and raw and real insights on how to sell more and make more!"

—Wally Kowis,
Captain of COOLTURE, Realty One Group

"I've been in business over 30 years, and every time I go to an S.O.S. event, I come away with completely new insights on the real estate business, at least 5 new ways to increase my sales and listings, and a Re-lit FIRE for SUCCESS!"

—Steve Decatur,
CENTURY 21, Recognized as a Top 10 Broker and Luxury Market Specialist

"I've been in business 10+ years, and Glenn's enthusiasm and authentic strategies for real estate set him apart! S.O.S. is a great program to be a part of. You always walk away with great techniques and tips for real estate sales success."

—Amy Walker Corey,
Keller Williams, Top Producing Team Leader

"Glenn is the real deal. Much like plugging in your electric vehicle for a charge, Glenn provides that charge for you as a REALTOR. To miss his content and attitude is to miss what's possible for your career and your life!"

—Coach Bill Hart,
Author of *White Collar Warrior*, Member of Movement Mortgage Leadership Team

"I have watched Glenn grow, give, and train. His enthusiasm for REALTORs is unmatched in his LIVE presentations! His insights on how to build a sales business are authentic and transferrable."

—Matt DeLaCruz,
Founder/CEO, The Winning Minds Group,
Aligned Mortgage Trainer/Coach

"Glenn's message delivered real, tangible solutions my salespeople could implement right now! Great creativity, thoughts, and ideas! He did an excellent job."

—Steve Jacobson,
President, *Fairway Mortgage*

"I have followed Glenn through his rise to becoming a Top 125 SUCCESS Influencer. His teachings are authentic and simple enough for anyone to grab this book and succeed! If you really want to accelerate your success and growth, go watch him LIVE; he is a BEAST!"

—Greg S Reid,
American Author & Entrepreneur

SOS

SOURCE OF SALES

A REALTOR's GUIDE TO INCREASING YOUR CONFIDENCE, CONVERSIONS, AND COMMISSIONS

GLENN BILL
#1 INTERNATIONAL BESTSELLING AUTHOR

UNIVERSITY
OF ATTITUDE

Copyright © 2022 Glenn Bill

All Rights Reserved. No part of this publication may be reproduced or transmitted in any form or by any means, mechanical or electronic, including photocopying and recording, or by any information storage and retrieval system, without permission in writing from the author or publisher (except by a reviewer, who may quote brief passages and/or show brief video clips in a review).

Disclaimer: This book is intended for entertainment and educational purposes only. While best efforts have been made in writing and publishing this book, the author and publisher make no representation or warranties of any kind and assume no liabilities of any kind with respect to the accuracy or completeness of the contents of this work. The advice and strategies contained herein may not be suitable for every situation. This work is sold with the understanding that the author and publisher are not engaged in rendering professional services. If assistance is required, the services of a professional person should be sought.

First Edition 2022

ISBN: (epub) 979-8-9858022-0-7

ISBN: (paperback) 979-8-9858022-1-4

Printed in the United States of America

Published by:

University of Attitude

6325 Guilford Ave Ste #203

Indianapolis, IN 46220

Cover and Interior Design by Rory Carruthers Marketing

Book Launch by Rory Carruthers Marketing

www.RoryCarruthers.com

For more information about **Glenn Bill** or to book him for your next event, speaking engagement, podcast, or media interview, please visit: **www.GlennBill.com**

To My Wife Colleen
for all the unanswered calls, missed dinners, and all the other chaos this crazy business demands of us. You were always there supporting me.

To all the spouses of REALTORs
for your patience, understanding, and acceptance of all these demands and still choosing to stay!

CONTENTS

Preface	xiii
Introduction	xv

PART I
SELF MASTERY

1. Self Mastery	5
2. Rules of Self Mastery	15

PART II
PROSPECTING MASTERY

3. Active Prospecting	41
4. Why We Don't Prospect	55
5. Connect & Convert	67
6. FSBO - Fastest Source of Business Opportunity	75
7. The Open House	81

PART III
SELLER MASTERY

8. Engagement Questions	91
9. Setting the Table with Sellers	99
10. Seller Attitudes and Perceptions	109
11. The Net Sheet - Your Best Tool	115
12. Seller Objections	123

PART IV
BUYER MASTERY

13. Setting the Table with Buyers	133
14. 21 Ways to Provide Service	141
15. Influencing Your Buyers	151
16. 21 Ways to Build Loyalty	159
17. Closing the Sale	167

PART V
VALUE MASTERY

18. Give Value First   177
19. Build Trust   189
20. Branding Yourself   193
21. 21 Ways to Beat the Commission Objection   203

Conclusion   213
Recommended Reading   215
Acknowledgments   217
About the Author   221
Notes   223

FIND, DEVELOP, AND MASTER YOUR CAREER

Dear Friend,

Congratulations on taking action to improve your life and career. This book will serve as your guide to finding, developing, and mastering YOUR Source of Sales.

I have dedicated my life to the fields of Real Estate Brokerage and Personal Development. Source of Sales has the best of what I have learned, experienced, and lived through since I began a career in this business in 1988.

I am certain that your quest for mastery will be accelerated after you accept and go through this challenge. The purpose of any goal or challenge is not what you get from it; it is who you become in the pursuit and accomplishment of it.

Inside this book, you will learn the secrets, scripts, and anecdotes that will allow you to begin to dominate your marketplace as well as transform your life with the greatness you have within you.

It is with heartfelt gratitude that I share this information with you. I hope that it will enrich your life and increase your productivity in your business.

This content is truly original, from the heart of a real estate practitioner just like you, one who was starved, disappointed, rejected, made fun of, and doubted, yet always believed in his Source.

I now invite you on the journey to find yours.

Welcome to the SOS Challenge,

Glenn Bill

**Founder,
University of Attitude**

PREFACE

Every REALTOR desires the same thing—to SELL MORE and MAKE MORE year over year without additional time, stress, and frustration. Most REALTORS and Brokers won't share what actually works because they are fearful of losing business. In fact, many intentionally give incorrect information leading you down a path to financial heartache. I know what it is like to search for the answers that no one is willing to give. Lucky for you, sharing the fundamentals of real estate sales is my passion!

The information I am sharing in this book quite literally changed my life. I have dedicated the majority of my life to developing the Source of Sales process. I have smashed over 30 years of real estate sales training into this book. These tips, secrets, and strategies made me millions of dollars and continue to make me millions more every year. I was dead broke before I developed the SOS process and have since enjoyed the millions the real estate industry has provided.

Within these pages, you are receiving the gift of the best buyer and seller questions along with tools to help close more deals and get more commissions in your bank account. You will achieve what most real estate agents only dream of by using the guaranteed strategies that I share to create a real estate business worth owning instead of one that owns you.

Reading SOS increases your comprehension of this amazing business known as real estate sales, putting you on a path to becoming a true professional of selling. You are building a skill set that sets you apart in your local marketplace and makes you an agent everyone wants to do business with. You are in the greatest business in the world. I believe anyone can make it in this business, especially if they follow the Source of Sales process step-by-step.

In the following pages, you are going to learn all about the Five Pillars of Success in the sales business:

- Self Mastery
- Prospecting Mastery
- Seller Mastery
- Buyer Mastery
- Value Mastery

Whether the market is booming or busting, the skills, attitudes, and strategies that you learn in this book are designed to keep you healthy in any market. The answers are all here. You just need to open your heart and mind and embrace what has worked for me and thousands of others who have studied the Source of Sales process.

My deep desire and solemn wish is that this book gives you the freedom you have been seeking, the validation you have been working so hard for, and the great accomplishments you know lie inside you. If you know, develop, and execute your SOURCE of SALES, your desire will become a reality.

INTRODUCTION

My Journey

I like to think back to when I became a new agent. I love new agents because they are high on enthusiasm and low on knowledge. That was me, many years ago, when I first met a man named Dusty Asberry. Dusty loved sales, he loved his company, he loved his product, and he loved his customers. Dusty did not have the most glamorous job in the world, but he understood this: You don't have to love your job, but you do have to love the way you do your job, and he loved the way he did what he did.

Dusty showed me my first apartment. He said, "Wow, Glenn, look at this step-saver kitchen. There are brand new doorknobs on the cabinets for you. And this faucet has been cleaned." Before I had time to absorb everything, he said, "Hey, let's go look at the bathroom!"

Dusty made me feel like that place was heaven. His enthusiasm for his product was contagious. I watched Dusty demonstrate real estate. Man was he good! Later, he said, "Glenn, you know what, I like you," and went on to offer me a job. He was looking for a leasing agent for all his apartments

Introduction

through Van Rooy Properties. Van Rooy owned about 1,000 apartments. They were currently at about 75%. They needed one guy to go around to their properties and lease them. I said, "Okay, I think I can do this, but I want to be paid $200 for every unit I lease." Dusty told me that wasn't how it usually worked, but they would agree to do it anyway.

I thought to myself, *how am I going to get people to lease these apartments?* I figured, **_free groceries_**! How many people would look at an apartment if they could get free groceries? I developed a program with a great local grocer, Breitbach's Foods, where I'd get $300 worth of groceries but only paid $150. We ended up renting about 100 apartments. Eventually, we got Van Rooy's occupancy to 98%. Needless to say, when I got my paycheck at the end of the month, they said, "What in the hell is going on?" **Lesson #1 in sales - create programs no one else can, no one else will try, and no one else will execute.**

Dusty got me started, but how did I get to where I am today, so many years later? Innovation, opportunity, enthusiasm, a positive attitude, and passion are certainly a few reasons I'm always selling.

What is selling? There are many different definitions, but I've always preferred this one: Selling is not telling; it is creating options and alternatives that give the customer feelings of certainty and significance, which culminates with ink on a piece of paper.

I had an opportunity to interview at several real estate companies when I started in the business. I was 19 with a wife and child, not the best prospect for an agent. I was denied by the FC Tucker Company, the largest independent in our market. They said, "You can't do it. You are in school. You are too young." I went to the Graves Company, the second-largest independent in our market, and they said, "You're in school. You are too young. You can't do it." I went to several other companies, independents, and discount brokers who said, "We

Introduction

don't want you." I finally had a little broker take a chance on me. That was all I needed—the chance to prove myself. Maybe you do too?

Trust me, I had a lot to prove. I started out in real estate with a two-door 1977 Ford Fairmont with red, plastic seats. As I would prospect, I would park my car around the corner and go door-knocking all the way around the block until I got back to my car. I had absolutely no money. I had absolutely no knowledge. However, about one and a half years later, through prospecting, I became the number one listing agent in our company at the age of 21.

I was serious about owning my own company. At 23, I became an owner within a large national franchise system. Along with my two partners, Steve Decatur and Tim O'Connor, I ran it for seventeen years. We started with sixteen agents and grew it to over one hundred and forty agents. We made nine-plus million in revenue and merged with one of the greatest sets of broker-owners, Mr. Mick Scheetz and Tracy Hutton. Mick and Tracy had passion, class, character, integrity, and professionalism, along with a wonderful team who helped support me in this incredible creation called Source of Sales. I've had a lot of success in real estate, and I know you can too!

The Source of Sales Challenge

I don't know how you're doing in your career in real estate, but my goal is to help you sell and market differently, create sales in half the amount of time, and get excited and passionate about your plans for a successful sales career. Don't fool yourself; you are in the business of sales and don't let anybody tell you any differently. One of the biggest mistakes I see agents make is trying to redefine the business; there is no redefinition. You are in the real estate sales business. That is why "sales" is in the title.

Introduction

Wherever you are now, or wherever you started, did you have it harder than I had it when you started? Would you agree that if I can do it, you can do it? There's no question that you can. Why do I get to write a book? I can tell you why - I really studied this stuff and have used it successfully for many years. I also love to coach, train, and give back when I can. I can assure you of this: I'm not better than you. You will be able to do everything I did when you learn the words, phrases, and techniques I share with you in this book.

As you go through this journey, I'll present you with many questions and resources. You must take the time to answer the questions and understand the SOS tools provided within this book.

To help you with this, I've created the *SOS Playbook*, which includes helpful exercises that relate to each part of the book and provides you with space to take on the SOS Challenge! Do not move from one part to the next until you complete the exercises. Do your best to follow along and write in the answers for expanded awareness and comprehension. Visit www.glennbill.com/sosplaybook to download your copy of the *SOS Playbook*.

I created The Source of Sales Challenge to help you expect more. I'm hoping that you want to double your income. When it's all said and done, I want you to finish this book and say you made ten grand plus. I believe that if you really embody this book and training, you can make $100,000 more, even $250,000 more. I've seen it happen with many of my students.

I want to give you ideas and thoughts to help you make another $100,000. You get what you expect out of yourself and others. That's in relationships, that's in friendships, that's with buyers, that's with sellers. The question is, what are you expecting?

What are you doing before you perform? How are you showing up with your clients? Have you ever seen the

Introduction

wealthiest people in the world show up at their job? They are called entertainers and professional athletes. Look at the rituals they engage in before they take the field. Do you perform a ritual that raises your emotion and energy before you get face-to-face with a prospect? If you are having unemotional, dull, and passive conversations, it's because you are unemotional, dull, and passive. You get what you give; never forget that.

Motion creates emotion. Real estate is the most emotional sale in the world. It is important to be emotional. I have this little chant - I learned it from my first mentor in this business, Tom Hopkins, "I'm alive, I'm alert, and I feel great." It might sound like something you'd chant with kids to get them pumped up. Sometimes we need to be kids; stop being a grown-up in this business. Today is the most important day of the rest of your career, and it's important that you understand the energy of emotion.

How are you starting your day? How are you starting your sales day every day? Do you wake up in the morning and say, "Good morning, God!" or do you wake up in the morning and say, "Good God, it's morning!" Do you say, "I need coffee to start my day!" Worse yet, do you believe that? The idea is that you do something each day that gets you excited and moves you forward. I don't care what it is, but you find it today.

To get you excited and move you forward, read and re-read this book and work on the exercises in the *SOS Playbook* to stay focused on what you will find to be **YOUR SOURCE** of **SALES!** Remember to visit www.glennbill.com/sosplaybook to download your copy of the *SOS Playbook*.

PART I

SELF MASTERY

After over 30 years in the real estate sales game, the one thing I can assure you is the ability to master your emotions, your thoughts, your actions, your expectations, your accomplishments, your failures, your relationships, your family, your free time, your nights and weekends, and your ambition, discipline, and goals will be the complicated matrix that brings you the success you dream of.

In its simplest form, this is called **Self Mastery**. The following pages will give you an excellent start to **Self Mastery** by identifying the people, motivators, and desires that you can leverage to find **Self Mastery**, also known as your SOURCES to **Self Mastery**!

As you begin to find your Source of Sales, you must first find your sources of **Self Mastery**. There are hundreds of places to find your path to **Self Mastery**. No one will have the same path, and that is okay. My sources of **Self Mastery** should not match yours. Different strokes for different folks.

The important thing is this—You must always seek to improve yourself, understand yourself, identify what drives you, determine what hinders you, discover what motivates and demotivates you, and realize **Self Mastery** is a journey, not a destination.

Your success will be directly proportional to the level of **Self Mastery** you develop. I know that the most successful salespeople have the highest degree of **Self Mastery**. If you ever question this, I challenge you to find the top salesperson in your company and the worst salesperson in your company, interview them both, and see how different the conversations are.

Focus the questions on **Self Mastery** and self-improvement. Ask about what they read, watch, and do to increase their command, control, and understanding of themselves. You may even want to interview yourself first!

Knowing where you are is a key to your personal mastery. Here are some tips for your self-interview:

1. How many transactions have I done in my career, this year, this quarter, this month, and this week? (After SOS, it should be 52 annually.)
2. How many followers do I have on my Facebook, Snapchat, TikTok, LinkedIn, and Instagram pages?
3. Do I send a monthly email and mailer to every sphere contact?
4. How many top-tier people do I have who like me, trust me, and refer me to business?
5. Do I have a marketing plan to engage with my sphere?
6. Do I have a bulletproof listing presentation? (You will after this book!)
7. Do I have a system to sell buyers in 10 showings or less?
8. Do I have a plan to create local celebrity in my business?

9. Do I have a vendor referral program?
10. Do I love what I do?
11. Do I run my business, or does my business run me?

You may not know the answers to all the above questions, but by the time you are done reading SOS, you will be able to answer all of those questions with confidence.

The following chapters on **Self Mastery** will give you a great start—a great opportunity to create a plan and a great source for **Self Mastery**!

1
SELF MASTERY

"Before you master others, you must first master yourself."
—Buddha

Who do we have to master in our real estate business? Buyers, sellers, appraisers, inspectors, loan originators, title reps, closers, contractors, underwriters, sales managers, trainers, new agents, old agents, the list goes on and on. For most agents, the other people we must master are the second half of the equation for greatness. If you haven't mastered yourself, how can you master others?

The most important relationship you must manage in this wonderful business is the relationship with yourself! "It's all about your relationships," you've heard it a million times. Unfortunately, if your relationships suck, your real estate career is going to suck too. The most important relationship (the one between you and you) is the one I hope you will choose to focus on first.

To influence and master other people, you first must master yourself. Buddha said, "You yourself, as much as anybody in the entire universe, deserve your love and affection." The bottom line is that you deserve to love yourself.

If you don't love yourself, your dreams, goals, past, and future, you will never get your clients to love you. So, from today on, stop hating yourself and start loving yourself and your future.

What Is My Source of Sales?

How do you master yourself? Find your source. What source gets you in your right mind and body? Your most important question for success is, **what is my Source of Sales?** Why do people do business with me? Why do people choose me over others? Answering those questions is how you discover your source.

Knowing your source is monumental to your career. I encourage you to put your thoughts and heart into answering these questions. This work is not easy. For some of the questions, you may think, "I have no idea. I've never asked myself these questions, and I'm clueless." That is why you have the exercises in the *SOS Playbook*.

What are the three reasons people do business with you? Many of the questions I ask you do not have a correct answer, so find the answer that's true for you. One tip would be to call your five best customers and ask why they do business with you.

Here's my next question: Are those three reasons good enough? Can those three reasons be improved? It's a challenge because I'm inviting you on a search to find three new reasons, three better reasons, that can help you dominate your competition.

Who Are My Three Best Mentors?

> *"When the student is ready, the teacher will appear."*
> —Tao Te Ching

SOURCE OF SALES (SOS)

Who are the people that create the source for you to get up out of bed and go into this crazy business called sales? You can list yourself, and that would probably be number one. Who else inspires you? Who are your teachers? What are you ready to learn today? What are you seeking? How much information are you seeking?

The more you seek, the more teachers will appear. Who are your three best mentors in your life? How much do you study them? Go to your *SOS Playbook* and write down the answers to these questions.

I want to introduce you to some of my sources. Each of them has taught me a lesson.

Mike Ferry: Mike is a real estate training business legend and my first mentor. In 1987, when I started real estate, I asked my broker, "What do I do?"

He gave me the *Superstar* Mike Ferry tapes. Mike Ferry simply taught me this: let's be brutally honest with people and tell it like it is. He also taught me that you get business if you talk to people.

Les Brown: I then picked up a tape from the great Les Brown. Les said, "If you take responsibility for yourself, you will develop a hunger to accomplish your dreams." My question: how hungry are you? Are you hungrier than your competitor? Are you hungrier than the people who are supporting you? Are you hungrier than the people you support? Being hungry in real estate sales is a fantastic thing. I wake up with tremendous hunger to succeed in our business.

"Live full, die empty."
—Les Brown

Hunger and emptiness correlate. They are both excellent motivators. Perhaps Les Brown agrees. He gave a speech called "Live Full and Die Empty." In it, he talks about how people go to their graves full of their hopes, full of their dreams, full of their ideas, and say, "I could have done this. I could have done that. I thought of that and never did anything."

To me, being empty in this quote means that you should not be afraid to try every brilliantly stupid idea you've ever had. Some people who practice this type of thinking end up billionaires. Full bank account and empty coffin! If you are hungry only when your stomach is empty, what does this mean? Both require a refill, a re-learn, a re-education; it's called growth. Hunger and being empty share one need— GROWTH (It is time to EAT)!

That's why I am glad you are reading this right now. You must be hungry. You have thoughts, dreams, and hopes inside you, so use them to feed your hunger and find your source.

Tom Hopkins: Tom Hopkins was the number one how-to sales trainer in the 70s and 80s in real estate. Tom was my first significant mentor. I was a very young salesperson, and Tom was coming to Indianapolis. I called his office and said, "Hey, I'd like to have dinner with the great Tom Hopkins." Tom was huge at the time. A dear friend of mine, Matt De La Cruz, was his promoter, possibly the best seminar promoter I have ever seen. He came and spoke at my office, sold a bunch of tickets, and arranged the dinner meeting. Imagine, a dinner meeting with my idol!

I went to this dinner with one hundred questions written on a yellow pad of paper. That meeting changed a lot for me. I helped Tom sell tickets to his events, and he helped me become a great sales trainer and speaker.

Is there somebody in your life that changed your life that

you haven't talked to yet? Is there somebody who makes you think, "Boy, I'd really like to be like them, but I don't have the guts to go talk to him."? Who do you need to reach out to and meet? Who could change it all for you? Who could be an added Source of Sales? Reach out to them. Help them sell more, and they will help you sell more.

Here's a challenge for you: pick somebody you know who could radically change your life for the better, call them up, and set an appointment with them. When you meet people who are important and successful, have questions written down. I had one hundred questions written down for Tom. That dinner took three and a half hours, and he had to speak to four hundred people the next day. He was so impressed, he asked me to introduce him at his seminar. Thus began my speaking career. I told him I wanted to be a speaker. Do you know what he said to me? "Oh God, Glenn, you don't want to be a speaker." Probably good advice, but I didn't listen!

Tom Hopkins has books called *Mastering the Art of Listing Real Estate*, which I devoured, *Mastering the Art of Selling Real Estate*, which I ate up, and *The Official Guide to Success*. Tom is a how-to salesperson.

Getting leads and clients is one thing. Knowing what to do and say once they are in front of you is another. These are the how-to skills that Tom and many others taught me, and now I am going to teach you.

Attorneys have language, doctors have language, architects have language, rappers have language, real estate people have a language, and salespeople have a language. There's a way to speak and communicate. Tom helped me understand what words I should use to get yeses and more yeses. Some describe Tom's training as a bit old-fashioned, but I can assure you that much of what he taught me still works today.

. . .

Floyd Wickman: Floyd is another legend in the real estate training field who started the Sweathogs Program. Floyd taught me that numbers matter. Know your numbers. With his program, you had to call one hundred people a day. We were cold calling; we were selling because we knew our numbers and had goals.

Jeffrey Gitomer: As you may know, I'm a Jeffrey Gitomer certified speaker and advisor. Jeffrey has written *The Little Red Book of Selling*, one of the best sales books in the world, and nine other best-sellers. I wasn't a professional speaker when his team found me and asked me to come and audition. Like *American Idol*, I flew down to South Carolina and met Jeffrey. Hundreds of people entered, and forty people showed up.

Man, you should have seen my audition; I was terrible. Michelle Joyce, his main marketer, looked at me after the audition with a very warm smile and said, "Have you ever seen a Jeffrey Gitomer book?" I remember saying, "Well...No." I think Jeffrey saw something in me and was gracious enough to let me re-audition after reviewing his material. They then gladly accepted me into "The King of Sales" world! He said, "Man, this guy is raw, real, and has some passion, so I want him to be my speaker." So, now I am.

They had given me an assignment that I did not really understand. I just knew I had the passion, attitude, and belief that I could speak. Maybe you should follow your heart, passion, and belief and not worry so much about the assignment at hand. To understand an assignment presented by another is good, but if you have no passion or original thought, you will fail. Be your original, authentic self. When you feel that, people will give you the benefit of the doubt and buy from you because you're honest, and honesty sells!

SOURCE OF SALES (SOS)

Who Would I Like to Begin to Study?

> *"People often say that motivation doesn't last.*
> *Well, neither does bathing*
> *- that's why we recommend it daily."*
> —Zig Ziglar

How extensive is your library? How many downloads do you have in your car that you listen to over and over again? Now you can even listen to podcasts in your car. It's not very romantic when I'm on a date with my wife, and we're listening to Zig Ziglar. I get it, but you've got to feed your mind constantly.

How much are you feeding your mind? Who are the three people you could study to make you a better person or salesperson? Write their names down in the *SOS Playbook*.

12 Areas of Study I Need to Develop

These are twelve studies of **Self Mastery**. How are you developing these?

Take ownership of:

1. Yourself
2. Your clients
3. Your financial freedom
4. Your happiness
5. Your attitude
6. Your example
7. Your motivation
8. Your vision
9. Your energy
10. Your belief
11. Your meaning

12. Your destiny

What Am I Really Willing to Do?

> *"Most people are not willing to do the hard work that makes sales easy."*
> —Jeffrey Gitomer

As a football coach, I was always fortunate enough to be asked to address our players at the height of big games. I've been lucky to be a part of thirteen state championship football teams. We'd always ask our players before they would take the field, *"What are you willing to do?"*

What are you really willing to do to be a champion? Being successful and creating these accomplishments isn't easy. Most people are not willing to do what it really takes.

What are you really willing to do to change and to create mastery? In your *SOS Playbook*, write down three things you're going to do that you haven't done. If you do, you will find the answer to this next question...

What Am I Fed Up with in My Life?

> *"The higher the threshold of uncertainty you are willing to take, risk, and deal with, the higher your sales and income will reach."*
> —Tony Robbins

You get to the point, the threshold of uncertainty, where you want to know what you will accomplish. I was very young when I started my career. As mentioned earlier, when I started driving in real estate, I had a gray, two-door 1977 Ford Fairmont with red vinyl interior; maybe the worst REALTOR car that was ever driven! Were you ever told you needed to

SOURCE OF SALES (SOS)

have four doors when you showed up at a home? When I began my real estate career, I was told that I needed a four-door sedan, updated, and newer, with leather seats preferably. Well, all I had at my disposal was my Ford Fairmont. I was like, "I'm sorry, let me move the seat for you, Mr. and Mrs. Buyer."

When I used to list property, I would park my car around the corner and door knock all the way to my listing appointments. My clients would ask, "Where is your car?" I would say, "I just wanted to talk to your neighbors and promote the listing." Truth is, I didn't want them to see my car. Another truth is neighbors talk, and they all said that no other REALTOR ever did that before. So, they all listed with me when it was time. A friendly door knock will always destroy a mailer. The problem is most REALTORs don't do either. Those that do always get business.

I was broke, working the third shift, and going to college. I was told by two real estate companies, "There's no way you can work a third shift, go to college, and do real estate." Are you in that spot right now? Are you feeling overwhelmed? Are you facing a whole lot of challenges? Are people looking at you in your office thinking, "That person has no chance"?

In real estate sales and professional speaking, my customers became endeared to me. Being hungry, humble, new, and young has its advantages; people want to help you get to the top. For all my customers from the beginning until now, I thank you, especially those who trusted in me in my first four years!

I soon graduated to a beautiful green Caprice Classic with the softest cloth green seats you would have ever wanted to feel and a soft leather top; I was so proud. The only problem was that it was old, had a lot of miles, and was a lemon! The air conditioning never worked, and on one hot, summer Indiana day when I was showing homes about fifty miles away from my marketplace, that sucker failed me big time! I can't remember the buyer's name, but she was sweet. I was maybe twenty-one, and I know she felt bad for me and gave me a chance.

We were out looking at farm properties, country homes, etc. While driving on one of these country roads, the A/C started blowing air. Not cold air, HOT, HOT air. Indiana summers are humid. Being a nice lady with lots of makeup and hot air blowing on you was not a good situation. My buyer, who I never saw again, had a melted face, was stuck fifty miles from her home in my broken car and had to call for help and be picked up on the side of the road. I had to learn the hard way that you get what you pay for. You will get punked if you buy impulsively and don't check things out. Mortified, I figured from then on, I'd only buy new cars!

The bottom line is there is a point where you get fed up. There's a point where you get pushed to your threshold. That happened to me when my daughter came along. True story, I went to check on her when she was in an in-home daycare. It was 1:00 in the afternoon, she had just finished lunch, and she had not had her face wiped. Snot everywhere, food everywhere, diaper full, and she smelled foul. I mean, it was gross. Seeing her like this changed it all for me. I held my daughter and said, "This shit is going to end. This is over. Nobody is going to treat my daughter like this."

I was fed up. That was a changing time in my life. I decided I would provide for my family financially because I couldn't take it anymore. My question is, what did it for you? What are you fed up with in your life? Use that as motivation to make a change for the better!

2

RULES OF SELF MASTERY

Personal development is not easy, but these rules will help you achieve **Self Mastery**. This chapter is filled with great reminders and resources. Once you've finished reading about these rules, don't forget to complete the exercises in the *SOS Playbook*.

Rule 1: YOU CAN'T DO IT ON YOUR OWN

> *"Each of us needs all of us, and all of us need each of us."*
> —Jim Rohn

You can't do it alone. Who is on your team? Who are you working with? We must work together to achieve our full potential in all areas of life. I learned this lesson when someone told me to stand and stretch my arms out as far as I could, so I did. Imagine this and what it looks like. He told the group to hold my outstretched hands and stretch out their arms and hands. What I saw was a doubling of my reach, not just on one side but two. Then he added a third link to this human chain, and I got the picture. You can only grow as far as your reach.

You can be the hub, but you will never grow if you are not attractive enough for people to attach to the end of your reach. Personal development is the seed for a heightened level of attraction. My guess is that if you have never studied personal development, you are not even close to being as attractive or as contagious as you can be. If you need people to sign orders to get you paid, I promise you these two qualities may be the best in sales.

Some people make you go, "Bam, I like him!" One example is Jimmy Fallon. People love Jimmy Fallon. Very, very popular. He's one of the most liked people in America. How does he do that? He is friendly, positive, and cares about his guests and audience. Some people create rapport within minutes. It's unbelievable; they can build rapport immediately. And you can too by learning how to get them talking.

Creating Rapport Within Minutes

1. What's your name?
2. Where are you from?
3. Tell me about your family.
4. What did your parents do?
5. Where did they live/come from?
6. What do you do for a career?
7. Do you love it?
8. What's the best thing about your career?
9. What are your hobbies?
10. What are you passionate about?

To attract a customer or recruit, you must first become attractive and build that rapport. How attractive are you to people? If nobody follows you, you're probably not a very

SOURCE OF SALES (SOS)

attractive person. You may be gorgeous, so people follow you, but is it due to your looks or persona? What value are you giving? Who are you leading? Other than looking great, what do you say, what do you do, or who are you becoming to be more attractive and popular?

In business, who are you leading? Are you leading your clients and customers? Or are your clients and customers leading you? If your clients and customers are leading you, you're not very attractive to them because you have no value.

Here are some examples of value that you can embrace and communicate:

1. Identify and solve their biggest challenge.
2. Have them give you their ultimate outcome and give them certainty that they will achieve it with you as a partner.
3. Help them in their business. Grow it, refer them to customers, and engage with their profession.
4. Create an exposure plan, quote how many eyeballs will be seeing their listing, and deliver.
5. Talk to them about how they understand and view time and how you can save them time.
6. Be a human, be kind, and empathize with what they tell you.
7. Be a trusted resource, not an "advisor" with everything related to real estate.
8. Teach them more than any other agent with statistics ready to go.
9. Prepare and have questions that go deep and get them to bond.
10. Don't be afraid of anything, have confidence, and be authentic.

I challenge you today to start leading people. Start leading your customers, clients, and other agents. Most importantly, start leading yourself because you'll find riches when you do.

People want to work with salespeople who lead them, who have credibility, who have superior market knowledge, and who have the guts to look them in the eye and say, "You are wrong" when they try and take the lead away from you. Telling a customer that they are wrong is one thing, eloquently demonstrating with examples and stories about how they are wrong is what sets the elite salespeople apart. How good are you at this?

Are you a real estate agent who goes around and begs for business? "Can I have a listing? Can I have a sale? I really need your business. Could you please refer me to somebody?" Begging does not work. You're annoying people, and that's not how you build a business.

You need to **monetize** your relationships by **giving**, not getting. To **get**, you must first **give**. The two most important feelings you must give are certainty and significance. These are the two emotional needs that people crave the most. The best salespeople I've ever seen know how to deliver these two emotional needs to people. How do you deliver certainty in your sales process? How do you make people feel significant during the sale? Read on to find the answers!

What value are you giving to the marketplace? Jeffrey Gitomer defines value like this: "It is what you do for the customer on behalf of the customer before you ask for the sale." The biggest issue with agents today is that they expect people to use them just because they went and got a real estate license; they offer no value to the customer, the market, or the real estate business in general. Not a good way to attract customers.

One mechanism to add value to the marketplace is social media. What kind of value are you giving to your community? Social media is free. At a minimum, you should have a Facebook Fan Page/Business Page, LinkedIn, TikTok,

SOURCE OF SALES (SOS)

Instagram, Snapchat, Twitter account, and a YouTube channel where you're giving value. Do you have one? Do you have all three? If not, right after you finish this chapter, set up your free marketing channels and provide value to all the potential customers looking for it. There are apps like Hootsuite that can integrate the three or four platforms you are on, so it disseminates to all platforms simultaneously when you do one post. We will delve further into VALUE later in the book as it is one of the Five Mastery Pillars to Real Estate success!

Is there somebody in the world that you can leverage and monetize a relationship with that you don't know? I suggest you identify them, target them, approach them, engage them, and close them. This will be very hard if you do not understand how to achieve personal mastery and rapport-building techniques.

We're in the sales game. When you're out in public, have you ever thought, "I don't want to talk to anyone tonight, and I don't want to make any new friends."? The more friends you have, the richer you become in this business.

I want you to create a relationship with somebody you don't know because there's value in everybody. I heard someone the other day say, "Everyone you meet knows more about something than you do; your job as an excellent rapport builder is to find out what it is." Find that value from somebody you don't know. Ask them questions from the *SOS Playbook*, make sure you compliment them, and ask where they come from.

How often do you compliment a person after they say their name? If you want to build rapport, compliment somebody. Do you hate being complimented? Some people don't do very well with compliments. When somebody compliments you, just say, "Thank you," and compliment them back.

Have you ever met somebody of significance where you

said, "Wow, this person is incredible; I'm going to monetize this"? One technique I love is asking someone about their grandparents. If you want to create rapport or build relationships, ask people about their grandparents. It freaks them out because nobody has ever asked them about their grandparents. If you're in an open house, go ahead, "So tell me, what did your grandparents do?" They're going to go, "Whoa."

That is an engagement question. You want to be the type of real estate agent who talks to people, engages them, and gets them to say, as Gitomer taught me, "Nobody has ever asked me that question before." It's a study. It's an art. Would that make you stand out, or does that make you one of the crowd?

Rule 2: YOU NEED A VISION

"Your vitality in life is directly proportional to the vividness of your vision."
—Dr. John DeMartini

To increase your income and enjoyment, you must eliminate your distractions. I want to help you create your vision. In this section, we will work on a bit of vision creation. What is your plan for success? Are you excited about it? Are you thinking, creating, and living in your circumstances or vision?

I'm going to ask you some questions that will upset you. I want you to be ready to take down your walls and open your mind.

How often do you sit down and work on yourself, your vision, and write things down? Probably not very often because most people don't have time. Today, I hope you will say, "I'm going to do this!" I want you to take this seriously and play full out. If you have no vision, that's okay. This book is going to inspire you to start your vision. The purpose of a vision is to pull the most out of the whole you, not the limited you.

What is the whole you? Are you walking around with limitations: self-limiting thoughts, self-limiting identity, or self-limiting experiences? We don't really understand what lies inside us until we really understand what lies within us. Remember Les Brown's advice, "Live full, die empty." Don't die full of your dreams; don't die full of your hopes. Don't die full of your potential.

This is part of the SOS Challenge where you're going to think, "This is challenging because I don't think about my vision, and I don't think about the whole me." People don't just sit around and go, "Hey, what's my vision?" Today, right now, I hope you will begin to ask yourself that question more often than you ever have before. Your vision is the "end result" behind your "how to get there."

Your vision is not supposed to be realistic. We're salespeople, right? We all deal in fantasy, so use your fantasy muscles now. I want you to get whacked out and think about some craziness in your vision. Like one of mine is to own an NFL football team. I'm serious. Unreal, yes, but that's my vision. When it happens in your mind, and more importantly in your heart, you're going to go, "I can't do that!" You don't need to worry about it; just get the vision. Another thing Les taught me was "when the why becomes clear, the how becomes easy." At the end of your days on Earth, the last thing you want to be saying to yourself is, "I should have done that; look what I missed out on!"

It might not be something you presently believe you can achieve. I want you to understand that it doesn't need to be realistic, and you don't need to think you'll achieve it. People don't sit around and go, "Well, let me write down what I know I can't do or don't think about what I can do." That's why this is a challenge, and maybe you'll go blank and go, "Gosh, I'd never even thought about how great my life could be."

The more ridiculous your vision is, the better. I mean it when I say take down your walls and play full out. Your vision is meant to pull you out of your comfort zone. As you're writing in your *SOS Playbook* about what you want your vision to be, you should be uncomfortable. If you're not uncomfortable, then that's a weak vision. I want you to think, "I really shouldn't put this." It's going to expand who you are. This is not an easy process. Let's find answers to the beginning of living full, dying empty. First, say this mantra, "I am comfortable being uncomfortable."

If you had your life to live all over again, would you do more with your life than you've done thus far? This is about realizing that you could have done more, and you can do more. Two people sit in your chair today. There is the person you are and the person you dream of being; both sit in that chair. What are you willing to do to be the person you dream of being?

I can tell you that the first step to becoming the person you dream about is writing down what that looks like to you. You can call on your vision no matter how ridiculous or stupid you think it is.

How are you going to access your vision? What lies within you that is different from most people? What are you aiming for? Do you aim high and miss or do you aim low and hit, or do you not aim at all? Are you aimless in your life? Are you just walking through and going, "I hope I can make this happen"? You might be thinking, "This is too big. I don't deserve it." Yes, you do deserve it. Don't hold yourself back. Have fun. Write it down in your *SOS Playbook*. If it seems ridiculous, you're onto something.

At this point, you might be wondering, *how is Glenn able to achieve such a high level of success?* I have a very vivid vision of what I expect to be, what I expect to do, what I expect to have, and you know what, I'm fired up about that. The great thing is you can be too. I don't know how vivid your vision is, but I can tell you that people who are depressed have no vision. People who are unenergetic have no vision. They have no idea what they are doing. They are ZOMBIES walking through life, and you can see them on the street, in the mall, or maybe even in your own home.

The great thing is you have a choice now. Today, you have a choice to move from uninspired and unmotivated to inspired and motivated. Get to that place where you think, "I've got a vision I'm working on. Every single day, I'm working on that." What is your vision? What do you work on every day? What gets you out of bed and helps you say, "Good morning, God."

When you have a clear vision, magnetic things occur. You're drawn to your life and have amazing synchronicity with people, places, things, and events.

> *"What great things would you attempt
> if you knew you could not fail?"*
> —Robert Schuller

Think about that. What would you do with your life and with yourself if you had all the money in the world?

Many years ago, Jeffrey Gitomer appeared in my life. I wanted to be a $1 million speaker. That's a goal. That's a vision. I want to make $1 million a day. I remember sitting at a Tony Robbins event with 4,000 other people who paid $2,000 a ticket. That's $8 million a day. I probably set my vision too low! I'm looking around, "That dude just made eight million bucks today?" Well, I said to myself, "I like this speaking thing." Then out of the blue, the number one bestselling author of *The Little Red Book of Selling* calls and says, "I want you to become a speaker for me." I auditioned. That's crazy. How did that happen? Vision. Write it down, dream bigger, seek, and find it.

How many times in real estate have you been experiencing financial pressure and stress, and then, boom, a sale comes? It's called synchronicity. It's all about your vision.

I think it's important that everybody aspires to be a multimillionaire. Jim Rohn's mentor Doctor Shoaff once said, "Set a goal to become a millionaire for what it makes of you to achieve it. Do it for the skills you have to learn and for the person you have to become." Goals are not meant for the end; it's about what you become because of the goals.

As you write your visions down in your *SOS Playbook*, it's not about achieving them. Everybody's happy with the money, but they're not happy with themselves. Pro athletes and entertainers have all the money in the world, and then they throw it all away. Why is that? Their goal might have been to make ten million, and they hit their goals. They're happy with the money, but they're unhappy with themselves. Your goals and vision are about who you have to become. For you to make one million, what type of person do you have to be?

If you do not have a vision, you're living someone else's. Are you living your vision, or are you living someone else's? Are you living your spouse's vision? Or is it your kids' vision? Some people let their kids run them. Maybe it's your sales manager's vision. Whose vision are you living?

Creating Your Vision

Dedicate one week and a set time to work on the questions below. Doing so will give you a great start. Each question should only require a focused, energetic mind for 30 minutes to answer. Remember that a vision is fluid and can change in minor adjustments or significant shifts. The point is to relax when it comes to vision setting and remember it is about the process, not the result.

SOURCE OF SALES (SOS)

1. When I look at my life in 1, 3, 5, and 10 years, what vision brings me calmness, fulfillment, and a sense of certainty about who I am and what I am here for?
2. When I look at my life in 1, 3, 5, and 10 years, who are the people I want around me? Who do I need to meet and form a better relationship with? What type of values and goals do they have for their life?
3. When I look at my life in 1, 3, 5, and 10 years, what do my surroundings look like? (Houses, locations, possessions, and material objects.) What do I own?
4. When I look at my life in 1, 3, 5, and 10 years, who have I influenced positively? What organizations have I served? Do I have my own organization or charity that contributes and gives back to society, or do I actively engage in another charitable organization to make a difference?
5. When I look at my life in 1, 3, 5, and 10 years, how do I physically look? What is my weight, body mass index, and strength level? How often do I train my body? What are my dietary intake and restrictions?
6. When I look at my life in 1, 3, 5, and 10 years, how much cash do I have in the bank and investments? What are my equitable assets and my actual net worth? Get your financial vision crystal clear; this is not the same as question 3.
7. When I look at my life in 1, 3, 5, and 10 years, how is my spirit? How is my emotional well-being? What do I do to stay balanced? Who are my mentors? How can I increase my involvement and engagement with the spiritual and emotional well-being that we all so desperately crave?

Rule #3 - Attitude

> *"It's your attitude, not your aptitude, which determines your altitude."*
> —Zig Ziglar

Jeffrey Gitomer's definition of attitude: the way **you** dedicate **yourself** to the way **you** think. How are you dedicating yourself to the way you think? What attitude are you bringing to your office, your family, and your friends? Earl Nightingale said, "You become what you think about all day long." What are you thinking about all day long? When we talk about dedicating yourself to a good, positive, YES! ATTITUDE ™[1], you must dedicate yourself because, by nature, 80% of what you're thinking about is negative.[2] You've got to move that out.

One great way to do that is to engage with me on my award-winning podcast, the GAP (Get Attitude Podcast), where we interview major influencers and innovators weekly to give you a positive dose of attitude all in one simple place.

What's the number one most important trait of a salesperson? A good attitude. It's the number one most important thing, yet nobody studies it. You should be studying it daily. Study it, commit to it, dedicate yourself to it, focus on it, be aware of it, have an insight, be curious, and have emotional control.

When I was a baby in listing real estate, I became the number one listing agent in a 70-person company. I always asked clients why they listed with me, and they said I had a great attitude, and it was awesome. I didn't know what I was doing, but I had a great attitude. If you improve your attitude today, you will get more business because people are attracted to a positive attitude.

Here's something I always do for positive thought before I

SOURCE OF SALES (SOS)

walk into my real estate office. I want you to try one of Tom Hopkins' techniques: reach down and grab an imaginary zipper and go zip...zip.... "I am now in my positive shell, and anything negative will bounce off of me." Right before you get in your office, zip it up. People don't want to hear negative talk, thoughts, or beliefs. Believe it or not, clients and customers do not want to listen to your personal tragedies. Your fellow real estate agents don't care about your problems. Lou Holtz advised, "Don't tell your problems to people. 80% don't care, and the other 20% are glad you have them." They don't care, so don't bring that stuff to the office or your clients.

We must understand that while a positive attitude gives us a lot, not having one costs us. I never like to be negative, but you must understand, sometimes you have a horrible attitude, myself included, and it costs you. It costs you relationships, energy, and vitality.

The secret to life is the ability to control your emotions. How well are you controlling your emotions with a difficult customer, lousy service, or poor seminar? The ability to control your emotions is everything. Realizing that blew me away because I tended to be an emotional person. At times, I still am, but it's really helped me in my business not to become emotional. Was it easy not to become emotional when an appraisal came in low? Hell, no. People go nuts when an appraisal comes in low.

Do you control your emotions? When I coached high school football, I always noticed how emotional coaches got on the sidelines. The coaches who lost their tempers, yelled at the players, and had uncontrolled body language typically lost the game...and their players' ability to follow. Leadership lesson: stay calm and control your emotions because if you are crazy, the people who follow you will be too.

Jim Rohn was fantastic; he gave me the formula for being rich. Do you understand that rich people and poor people have the same amount of time in a day? Wouldn't that drive you crazy if you were poor? We've all got the same amount of time that rich people or successful real estate agents have. 15, 30, 100 million-dollar producers have the same amount of time a day as the $2 million producers.

What's the difference? I'm going to give you the formula. There are about a half-dozen things to make 80% of the difference. There are about five or six things that make a difference in your health, five or six things that make a difference in your education, five or six things that make a difference in your income, five or six things that make a difference in your success as a real estate salesperson. They make 80% of the difference.

Those who keep looking for the few things that make the most difference are the winners. So many of us think we know five or six things. But the quest is: refine it, refine it, refine it. What are the five or six things that really make 80% of the difference? How much time are you spending on them?

In my career, I've come up with seven crucial things that have made all the difference in my level of success. Here are my suggestions on the seven most important things in real estate sales:

1. Meet face-to-face with sellers.
2. Do net proceeds demonstrations for them.
3. Get listing agreements signed.
4. Interview buyers face-to-face.
5. Show them properties with payments and cash to close ready.
6. Have them sign purchase agreements.
7. Set more appointments with people who need to buy and sell.

Successful people spend their time on these seven things, not everything else that doesn't really matter. Look at your business, look at yourself and say, "What am I really doing here?"

How's your attitude working for you? In my book, *The ABC's of ATTITUDE*, I address pivotal questions. This is a question that we are constantly asking ourselves as we go through life; when we are presented with a major decision in our life or in times of great stress, this is the question we ask ourselves. My pivotal question is, "How can I move people from can't to can in a loving and constructive manner?" What's your pivotal question?

That's where it all starts. Your pivotal question drives your attitude. Ask the wrong question, get the wrong answer. Are you asking yourself the wrong questions? Are there better questions you can be asking yourself about your business, your life, and your relationships? The best thing Jim Rohn ever said was, "Attitude drives actions. Actions drive results. Results drive your lifestyle." If you think your lifestyle is not great, you really need to look at your results. If your results are great, you really need to look at your actions. If you don't like your actions, you probably need to look at your attitude. If you think your attitude stinks, then your philosophy probably stinks too.

What Is the Cure?

- Daily study - How about ten minutes a day?
- Commitment - How about first thing in the morning, every morning?
- Dedication - How about listing those people who are dedicated to you and honoring them?
- Focus - How about doing this in an absolute vacuum with no cellphone, no music, no nothing?
- Awareness - How about taking an inventory of

where you are, where you've been, and where you are going?
- Insight - How about studying others who are successful in areas you want to be in five minutes per day?
- Curiosity - How about writing ten quality questions for every important meeting you have before the meeting?
- Emotional control - How about already seeing yourself succeeding and feeling what it looks like? Most importantly, begin feeling that if it doesn't go well, you will reframe your disappointment into a positive and leverage it to give you more passion, more insight, and more power!

Three Attitude Killers

1. People who...

- did you wrong. If I had a theme song for this, it would be, "Hey Won't You Play Another Somebody Done Somebody Wrong Song." Somebody did you wrong; that's an attitude killer. An appraiser or a buyer who bought a For Sale By Owner without you, or a seller who listed with a guy because his fee was less. We're going to erase all that. People who do you wrong should be looked at as gifts. Why? You'll never have to deal with them again, you'll never fall for the same type of game they play, and lastly, because it will force you to look for quality people to do business with instead of accepting anyone as a client.
- are bad examples. People who you look to who have crappy attitudes can be attitude killers. Don't

SOURCE OF SALES (SOS)

take advice from someone more messed up than you!
- you're married to and work with who have bad attitudes. They're attitude killers. If you're married to someone with a bad attitude, help them out. If you're working with someone with a bad attitude, help them out. Negative attitudes drain your energy. They prolong painful situations. A bad situation lasts ten minutes; a person with a bad attitude lasts forever. They block positive and creative thoughts.

2. Thoughts that...

- drain your energy - I am exhausted, overworked, destined to fail.
- prolong painful situations - physical health problems, relationship breakups, etc.
- block the positive - Why am I doing this? Will I ever succeed? Should I be doing something else?
- take the fun out of life - I don't enjoy doing new things. I am not interested in improving what I know and have. I am not aware of how great and fun selling can be.

Do you stay angry for more than an hour? Let's stop that. What's it doing for you? Is it making your life better? Is it making you more profitable by being angry for more than an hour? I can give you an hour, but I would encourage you to stay upset for only ten minutes because you block creative thought and the ability to grow and do things for other people when you keep a bad attitude.

3. Things that happen that can make you angry...

- Falling sales. We must learn to see falling sales as a great learning experience and an opportunity to work on your sense of humor.
- Lousy service. I get impatient fast, but I've begun to understand that lousy service doesn't mean lousy person. A big help in this area is to imagine or think about the lousy day the person who has given you lousy service is having or how that day started. They will love your empathy, and I bet they will improve your service.
- Overindulging. Look, nobody loves to overindulge more than me! Whether it be alcohol, food, negative thought patterns, prospecting, not prospecting, excuse-making, I think you get the picture. Whether the task is positive or negative, overindulgence can handcuff your success and speed to greatness. Do you overindulge? If so, determine where it happens and change your mindset about it NOW!
- Not being able to pay your bills. Poverty is a definite buzzkill. My suggestion is to NOT focus on being broke but on getting your next appointment, achieving the next small goal, and focusing on the future. Focusing on poverty will only get you POVERTY!

Three Attitude Solutions

1. Be nice. You'd be amazed at what that will do for you.
2. Get involved with something bigger than yourself.
3. Don't worry; be happy.

Be kind. Smile. Make friends. We should be making

friends every day. Say nice things to people. Praise other people. It's amazing in a real estate office; somebody gets a new listing, people are like, "Hey, he probably bought the listing." Right? Try this: "Hey, great listing!"

Take responsibility. Quit shifting blame or compliments and recognize others' accomplishments and greatness in your office or life. Be proud of your work and the work done by others. Be proud of your accomplishments.

Rule #4 - The Recondition Process

Understand and crave the reconditioning process. There's a word called refinement when you talk about leadership and success. Those who are willing to refine themselves and recondition themselves monthly or quarterly are the people who lead and make a lot of money.

First, you have to crave it. You have to say, "I want to be better. I am not satisfied." Be blessed with dissatisfaction. I'm never satisfied. You should never be satisfied. There's always more to do. There's always more to be done. There's always more to have. Be blessed with dissatisfaction.

First Step - Know your outcome. If you want to change your outcome, you need to know your outcome instead of aimlessly getting through each day. Clarity is power. If you want to lose weight, you need to have a clear outcome. You can't just say, "I'm going on a diet." That isn't effective. What is your specific goal?

How clear are you on your outcome in your business? How clear are you on your outcome with your relationships? How clear are you on your outcome with prospecting? How clear are you on your outcome with listings and buyers?

Buyers and sellers want one thing, and it's called certainty. You know what? Most people want certainty in their life. As a real estate professional, the more certainty and the more clarity you give people, the more you're valued, the more they want you in their life, the more money they will give you.

Second Step - Ask yourself the four questions for reconditioning. I always ask myself these four questions:

1. Why?
2. Why not?
3. Why not me?
4. Why not now?

Third Step - Check your beliefs. We all have beliefs. What do you believe? The biggest problem in relationships is people believe two different things. The biggest problem in real estate, with our clients, is buyers and sellers believe two different things. Sellers believe that we make too much money. Sellers believe that we don't understand the market data. Buyers believe that we have nothing else to do except wipe their noses and show them homes. We believe that we need to be at the lowest, most competitive price to get the highest numbers. Check your beliefs about the following things.

What do you believe about your career? Is your career fulfilling? Is your career paying you what you want it to? Does real estate stink, or does it not stink? Do you believe your career is the absolute greatest career you could ever be in? I can't imagine *not* being in the real estate business. The thought of working for someone else makes me nauseous. We have the greatest job in the world.

. . .

SOURCE OF SALES (SOS)

What do you believe about your relationships? Do you believe your relationships are strong? Are they caring? Are they delivering what you want?

What do you believe about yourself? Do you believe that you don't deserve all the success you should have? Do you believe that you've only hit the tip of the iceberg? Do you believe that you have no vision or don't deserve a vision?

What do you believe in about your company? Hopefully, you love your company. If you don't love your company, leave and find another one.

What do you believe about your service? I believe my service is second to none. I believe that I'll respond to an email or a text within two minutes, no matter what the time. Other people believe that you're cutting out your family if you do that. Other people believe that if you give that level of service, you're cheating somebody. I'm here to tell you that that's what they believe. Check your beliefs in all these areas and make sure that what you believe is helping you instead of pulling you down.

What do you believe about your results? Do you believe your results are your 1099? Do you believe that your results meet your expectations? Do you believe that your results are good enough, or do you believe they're too low? Do you believe that your results are a motivator? Do you believe that your results are a de-motivator?

. . .

Perhaps the greatest question to ask yourself about your beliefs: Are they true?

> *"If you ain't failing, you ain't trying."*
> —Nick Horton

Your view of failure needs to be reconditioned. You will learn more about this in Part Two: **Prospecting Mastery**. I love to fail. I am not afraid of failure. I must risk failure in order to grow, or I wouldn't put myself out on a line and publish this book. When you're prospecting, when you're growing your business, when you're looking at personal growth, you have to fail.

Fourth Step - Leverage your Empowering Inner Voices. People ask how I stay driven. I set goals and create a vision in order to possess the drive. If you're lacking motivation, if you're lacking drive, if you feel like you're helpless, if you're not excited about your career, it will indicate only one thing to me - you have no goals. You don't have to love your job, but you have to love the way you do your job. You don't have to like it; like the way you do it.

You may not like real estate but fall in love with how you do real estate. When you start falling in love with the way you do your business, you're going to find that you're going to make a lot more money. That's what this book is here to do; get you to do your business differently, get you to think differently, "How can I do my business, so it's better?"

We need to recondition our view of prospecting. "I must create and follow a plan for both active and inactive prospecting to dominate listings and sales."

SOURCE OF SALES (SOS)

Fifth Step - Take Massive Action

"The path to success is to take massive, determined action."
—Tony Robbins

The path to success is to take massive action. What massive action have you taken recently? What massive action could you take in your future in your sales career? I took Massive Action, I'm a graduate now of Tony Robbins University, and I learned an awful lot.

Five great ways to take Massive Action:

1. Spend the money and invest in yourself.
2. Take the time, whether it is daily, weekly, or monthly, to do something you are not doing now to better your business. Classes, activities, challenges, watching trainings on YouTube, listening to podcasts, the list goes on.
3. List the three things you have been wanting to do and complete them before you do anything else.
4. Punish yourself if you do not complete #3. Maybe set up a partner you pay $10,000 to if you do not complete your list of three.
5. See yourself and write what your life will look like after completing the massive action you know you should take.

Where can you take Massive Action in your life? In the *SOS Playbook*, you can identify areas of your life that require Massive Action. You'll also find the Stretch Your Expectations test, which will help identify your expectations, strengths, and areas of personal development.

Self Mastery
SOS Challenge

To begin Self Mastery, complete the exercises in the *SOS Playbook*. If you don't already have your *SOS Playbook*, visit www.glennbill.com/sosplaybook to download your copy.

To start applying the four rules of Self Mastery to your life, complete the exercises in the *SOS Playbook*. You will find two tests related to your attitude. These are questions you should be asking yourself to help you identify your attitude and areas of personal development.

PART II

PROSPECTING MASTERY

Perhaps the most important, valuable, and freeing mindset of a salesperson is a mindset that matches those men and women who traveled across the fruited plain in hopes of finding riches in gold!

Think about what those pioneers had to deal with: no car, no cell phone, no Google, no GPS, no bathrooms, no shower, no cable, no fresh clothes, no health care, no emotional support coaches, no lead gen sources, no automated responders, no AI, but they also had no excuses, no quit, no lack of desire, no lack of a dream, no absence of doubt when it came to getting rich and finding their treasure.

In today's world, everyone wants someone else to make the sales call, do the prospecting, create the lead. For God's sake, salespeople pay for leads, especially crappy leads, that close at 2%!

Could you imagine the gold rush people saying, "Can I hire you to go do the work to find the gold, and I'll pay you a referral fee?" Could you imagine people cold calling individuals and saying, "Pay me to go find some hot spots for your gold. No guarantee it's there, but you pay us anyway"?

Do you understand that when you pay people to prospect or cold/warm call for you, you are being cold-called yourself? Do you see salespeople getting cold-called and closed over the phone by lead gen organizations having their money taken only to see no return? If not, just scroll your Facebook and LinkedIn feed.

If you want to get rich in sales, you need to understand that the best Source of Sales, leads, wealth, accomplishment, self-satisfaction, and victory only comes from you.

If you desire to be the most profitable salesperson you can be, paying for leads is not the way to get there. In the following pages, you will see what I did as a nineteen-year-old salesperson to develop my business on my own for free. I had no money, no customers, and no belief that I could fail. If this describes you, you will love reading the next few chapters!

3

ACTIVE PROSPECTING

*"What people can do is very different
from what they will do."*
—Tony Robbins

When my son started driving, he and I drove downtown to a friend's house. I said, "Go to Keystone Avenue and start driving south. You'll notice that all the numbers will get smaller from 71st to 65th to 52nd. When you hit 46th, turn right. Did you notice how the numbers went down?" And what does he say to me?

"Don't worry, Dad. I'll just GPS it."

"Well, what happens if the battery runs out on your phone, and you have no GPS? What's going to happen?" What's he going to be? Lost.

This chapter is about understanding your directions. This chapter is about understanding where north, south, east, and west are in real estate. This chapter is about getting rid of the GPS and really understanding the essence of real estate sales.

The Mentality of Prospecting

There are a lot of tools, a lot of tricks, and a lot of great gimmicks that go on in real estate, but unless you have this piece down, you are going to be lost. I don't care what excellent marketing programs you have. If you haven't mastered the "mentality of prospecting," you will be lost. You will not be able to make money in an ever-changing market.

Prospecting Mastery helps you survive in great markets. It helps you survive in down markets. It helps you survive when your attitude is not good. It helps you survive when your attitude is great.

There is an overabundance of programs that prospect for you. I've never seen one work. I've never seen one (if it did work) be equitable and fair to an agent. The best prospector in your business needs to be you, period. If you follow SOS, you will need to pay no one, count on no one, and be held accountable to no one. This stuff was learned, created, and generated in the streets. It is authentic, real, and the fastest way to riches in the business.

In 1988, I was broke, working three jobs, was in college, and had a child. When I got into the business, I understood one thing: I needed to get in front of people and have them sign my two best friends: purchase agreements and listing agreements. I needed to get in front of people who could say yes to signing their names on these two forms. That is what **Prospecting Mastery** is all about.

I'm going to share with you in this chapter how the youngest person in the company became the number one listing and selling agent through understanding this concept known as **Prospecting Mastery**. I'm going to share with you more than thirty years of what I've done to generate business.

SOURCE OF SALES (SOS)

Active Versus Inactive Prospecting

I want you to understand two things: active prospecting and inactive prospecting. Active prospecting is when you go out, beat the bushes, and make things happen. Inactive prospecting is when you are in the marketplace, delivering value, and people are coming to you.

Inactive prospecting is becoming more prevalent now than active prospecting. You need to create an inactive way to prospect, which many today refer to as branding yourself and building value. However, there needs to be a balance between the two. You need to master both types of prospecting. When that pendulum swings, you need to be able to prospect actively. Active Prospecting is my personal favorite because it reduces the time between introduction and signatures.

Active Prospecting includes:

1. FSBO's
2. Expireds
3. Dilapidated property visits
4. Cold calls/Door-knocks
5. Garage Sale visits
6. Face-to-Face appointments

Inactive Prospecting includes:

1. Monthly postcards to past clients
2. Billboard or grocery cart ads
3. Sponsorships
4. Mailers
5. Facebook ads
6. No face-to-face activities

Why We Love to Prospect

> *"Anticipation is the electricity of childhood."*
> —Jason Kotecki

What if you start every morning in real estate going, "God, I love to prospect!"? Those who don't feel that way are poor real estate agents. They don't like to prospect; they like to sleep, and they are broke. If you went to a different market, could you tear it apart and be the number one listing and salesperson tomorrow? Or would you be lost, like someone without his GPS?

You might be new to this and need to figure out how to generate sales. I feel you. I've been there. When I was starting, all my friends were going to parties. I was underage. I had no referrals. I had to go into the market and make my way. You need to make your mark in your market.

Why do we love to prospect? I will give you a few reasons why you should love it. Let me start by giving you a clue on prospecting. Become a child! Have fun with it. Grown-ups make terrible prospectors. Kids who want something are good prospectors. Have favorable anticipation toward prospecting. It's about the mentality of a person who loves to prospect. I had nothing. My mentality was young and simple.

1. **It is our job.** Do you have at least four pending sales right now? Any agent in the business should always have at least four pending transactions. If you are an agent who does not, then you are failing to understand what your job is. Your job is to prospect until you get to your four pending transactions. Period. End of story.

I can hear you asking, "What about my pending

transactions?" Yes. I know about those. How long does it really take to get a pending transaction to close? Other than inspections, most details and monitoring take just five minutes a day. That is it! You should devote the rest of the time to contacting and prospecting future clients. Don't make the mistake of many agents out there who baby and nurse their deals, only to create more problems in those deals and give themselves a perfect excuse not to prospect. I love this saying, "REALTORS were the first people to make mountains out of molehills."

2. **Our <u>future in sales</u> depends on it.** If you do not prospect, you will have no future. This business will not work for you. If you sit and wait for business to come to you, you are doomed. That's not how this business works. You need to go hunt for some business. You eat what you kill.

The great Les Brown says, "You have to make NO your vitamin." I believe that, and I will show you later in the CACC Formula how that is true. If I don't sell enough, that's on me. I didn't hunt enough. It's time for us to become cavemen and women. Let's go hunt. Let's go eat. The number of sales you make is directly proportional to the amount of NO's you get. Keep trying.

3. **It gives us <u>momentum</u> and a feeling of accomplishment.** When you're down in real estate, what's going on in your real estate life? No closings, no listing appointments, nothing. Nothing's happening. All you're doing is getting self-absorbed and pitying yourself. Depression is when you focus on yourself and all the things you cannot get. We can

get depressed when we don't experience that momentum and success. When you say things like, "Well, I don't have...I don't get...it's about me, me, me," you're going to be depressed. I don't want you depressed. I want you to be the source of non-depression.

Real estate is the best career in the world. We can get dressed up, go to an office, sit at a desk, and have a phone and a secretary. We don't have to do anything. We can have coffee, and we can complain with our fellow sales associates about how the market is terrible. Then we can get in our cars and go to lunch together. Hey, it's lunchtime, all right! Then we can sit in the office all day and go, "God, it's floortime, oh good! Can you believe it? Not one person called me on the floor." Here's what I've figured out. Why would I wait three hours and take the floor if I could generate twenty contacts in the same amount of time and make business happen? I figured out floortime within the first week. I HAVE to work with people that call because it's a customer service issue. Am I going to wait on people to call me? No, I am going to make contacts.

The point is, if you're not out prospecting every day, you're not building your pipeline. If you have no momentum and you have no feeling of accomplishment, it isn't fun in this business.

When people ask you, "What do you do for a living?" I'd say, "Prospect." I don't sell real estate. We don't want to tell the public that, but I want you to say to yourself, "I'm a prospector. If I don't have four deals in the pipeline, I'm not in this business." Your business is

SOURCE OF SALES (SOS)

prospecting until you build up a consistent stream of at least 48 transactions a year.

Do you have momentum in your career? Every day, I accomplish something. The definition of work is when you're face-to-face with somebody who can say yes to you. Everything else is preparation. My litmus test in my real estate career is this: was I face-to-face with somebody who could sign a listing or purchase agreement? My deal is that every customer or client has to sign one thing every day. Price reduction, inspection amendment, listing contract, etc. Some form gets signed by somebody other than me. That's working in the business. If you are not getting signatures every day, you are not working. You are just preparing and planning.

4. **It prevents us from emotional and financial pitfalls.** We have all had financial pitfalls in this business. Too much month at the end of the money. "I'm two weeks short!" Prospecting will help you deal with that—no more pitfalls. There are super agents in your office who make 50 grand one month, then nothing the next. Make 30 grand one month, then nothing the next. Make 20 grand one month, then nothing the next; you get the picture. When I prospect, I make a bunch of money. When I don't prospect, I make nothing. Prospecting leads to a nice, consistent road map in your real estate career and your bank account!

5. **It is the single best way to build your Sphere of Influence.** Your Sphere of Influence is necessary for a referral-based business. How many people do you add to your Sphere of Influence every day in your

business? How do you define your Sphere of Influence?

Real Estate Sales managers and trainers always talk about your SOI (Sphere of Influence), your CRM (Customer Relationship Management), or your CMS (Customer Management System). Still, they rarely tell you who gets into this system and how they get into it. Well, look no further; I will give you the secret! The people who go into this system must qualify in three ways. They must

1. Like you.
2. Trust you.
3. Refer you business.

If they do not do all those things, they should not be in your business sphere.

The CACC Formula

Is there any reason why you can't close 48 transactions a year? The real question is, why aren't you? How many times do casinos check their numbers in Las Vegas? Every hour. Do you think Vegas knows their numbers? Yes. So how well do you know your numbers? To help you with this, I will give you one simple formula that shows you that if you talk to a certain number of people about real estate, you will make $100,000 per year!

SOURCE OF SALES (SOS)

CACC Formula
**Contacts - 1350
Appointments - 135
Contracts - 27
Closings - 23.8
Income = $125,000**

The first number you need to know is your desired income. Once you have committed to your desired income, you will work backward through the CACC Formula.

Looking at the formula above, the desired income is $125,000 in gross closed commission (that was one of my early goals). With an average sales price of $175,000 and an average commission of .03, the average commission is $5,250 gross.

With a $5,250 dollar commission, how many contacts do you need to make to have your desired income? Your job is nothing more than identifying how many contacts it takes to make money, then simply going out and identifying contacts to make and talk to. How simple is that? Well, the reality is the more you use the formula, the simpler it gets.

The next reality is this, you need to start with the end in mind and work in reverse to see how many contacts you need to make to get to your goal. It is very simple; if you make a certain number of contacts, you will close a certain amount of income. It really doesn't depend on your skill level, mailing list, database, or internet marketing program.

Know this—The average income of a REALTOR, based on NAR findings, is $52,000. This formula will allow you to double it. In reality, this formula allows you to 10x it if you desire. You can plug whatever your average sale price, commission or desired income is, follow it, and make those contacts!

. . .

So, to work the formula we must:

- Find out how many **Closings** we need to hit our income goal.
- Find out how many **Contracts** we must write to hit our closing goal.
- Find out how many **Appointments** we must go on to hit our contract written goal.
- Find out how many **Contacts** we need to make to set and hit our appointment goal.

Here is how to arrive at how many **C**losings we need (the last C in the formula):

The formula is this: **D.I. / A.C. = C**

Desired **I**ncome, D.I., is $125,000 divided by an **A**verage **C**ommission, A.C., of $5,250 = # of Closings needed. $125,000 divided by $5250 = 23.8. Let's call it 24 closings!

Can you believe that if you just close 24 transactions a year, you can gross close to $125,000 in this business at an average sale price of $175,000? I love it! Do you think you could manage to sell two homes a month to make $100,000? I think you can.

Let's continue to break down the formula. How many **C**ontracts do I need to write in order to gross close $125,000? Well, all you need to do is ask yourself, "For me to close 24 transactions, how many contracts would I expect to fall through?" Add them to your desired closings. I have found that one out of five transactions is more than enough leeway to give yourself when figuring fall-throughs.

As you study the SOS system, you will see fall-throughs reduce to more like 5%, but for now, use a 20% fall-through ratio; it will help you overachieve. If you do not get 20% fall-through and only have 5% fall-through, you will be making a lot more than your desired income. If you add 20% fall-through, that means you will need to write 30 transactions to hit your goal with no problem. It means you won't be stressed out if a transaction falls. It also means you can negotiate for your client and customer out of strength and not fear.

I was told, "get the dollar signs out of your eyes." Quite possibly the best advice I have ever been given about this business. I always focused on the numbers, the contacts, and the clients. I never counted commissions before closing. Sure enough, the deal was doomed from the get-go if I did.

You now know how to come up with # of Closings, and # of Contracts. Now it is time to figure out how many Appointments you need to go on.

I always figure worst case, we know that you need to write 30 transactions. Even the worst salesperson can close two out of ten appointments, so all we need to do is multiply desired written contracts by five (which is the factor for 20%), which means you need to go on 150 appointments. All you need to do to make $100,000 in this business is to get face-to-face with 150 people who want to buy or sell within a year. Is that doable? Is that harder than any other job you've ever had before? I doubt it.

But just in case you struggle as a salesperson, I've given you the lowest conversion. You can be a Neanderthal and do these numbers and make money. Trust me, I've seen it. I've worked with people who have made me think, "There's no way this person's going to make it." But man, they did the numbers, and people said yes to them because they understood what prospecting mentality means.

I need to schedule 150 appointments, and I need to close 30 of them. That gives me 24 contracts (or more if your sales ability is good and you study my training). Six contracts are going to fall through. I know if I can book 150 appointments, I'm on my way to making 100 grand.

The question is, how many appointments did you set last

year? Were you close to 150? You've got to know your numbers. The number one thing you do if you hire an assistant is have them schedule your time. I'm guessing you are in more than 150 appointments when it's all said and done.

I know that if I have 150 appointments and close 20% of them, I will end up with 24 deals that close. At a minimum, I'm going to make 100 grand. You can put in whatever number you want. If you want to make half a million, just work your formula.

Here's the deal. How many contacts must I have? I need 1500 contacts, divided by 10. So that means only 10%. One out of every ten people that I contact does business with me.

If you want to say it's 20, then divide by 5. You're going to increase that to 2600 contacts. If you have 1500 contacts, one out of every ten contacts you make, especially if you're calling FSBOs, expireds, and targeted contracts, you're going to get 150 appointments.

Next is **C**ontacts. I'm going to set a goal to make 1350 contacts. You will learn more about making those contacts later. You might be thinking, "1500? Wow." However, let me ask you a question. If I said to you, "I have a job, a position on my team. I'm going to give you a $100,000 a year salary. All you have to do is get dressed up and talk to 1500 people." That's not hard. If you contact 1500 people, that will lead to 150 appointments and 30 contracts. You will end up with 24 closings, and your income will be 125 grand.

If we break it down further, that equals 15 contacts in 100 days. There are 365 days in a year. So, it's all broken down for you. One hundred days a year, your job is to prospect. I need you to make 15 and a half contacts in 100 days. It's simple. That's 12 days a month. Half a month, you need to be out prospecting. Maybe it's every other day. Just imagine. What if you meet people and say, "Hi, what's your name? What a great name. You've got fantastic hair. I love it. Where are you from? That's interesting." What if you just do that for 100 days?

Social Media & Prospecting

Social media could blow these numbers away. I have 5,000 people on my Facebook page. If I post something because I want to market something, I can market to 5,000 people in one minute and be done. What if you add LinkedIn, Instagram, Snapchat, and TikTok?!

What can social media do for your contacts? Do you have your own Facebook Fan Page? Do you realize you can post quality content on there and build up your likes and build up your Sphere of Influence? Every open house, say, "Hey, look, I'm on Facebook. I value messages on my Facebook page. I'd love for you to like me. What's your name? I'll like you on Facebook." Maybe you run contests. Active prospecting, getting out, beating the bushes, and making it happen, is essential. However, you also need to understand how to build your social presence online.

Somebody called me and said, "Are you Mr. Bill?"

"Yes."

"I was just given your name by a lady who was our waitress at the pancake house."

"Wow, okay, how'd that happen? What was her name?"

"I can't remember. I think it was Tracy. Said she knew you in high school."

I hadn't talked to Tracy in 22 years. But I saw Tracy's picture on Facebook and asked if she wanted to be friends. She friended me back. Then she'll post stuff about her kids, and what do I do? I like it! Then she likes me back. I haven't talked to her in 22 years. But we're friends, and we like each other back and forth, bing, bing, bing. Like, like, like. Friend, friend. It's awesome.

I went to this listing presentation. I listed their home for

$186,000, charged them a full fee, and made $8,200 because of Facebook.

I have that story times ten. I make over $100,000 annually simply through Facebook. It's an excellent idea to connect with people on social media.

It is time to embrace prospecting. Set your goals using the CACC Formula, get on social media, and start making contact!

4

WHY WE DON'T PROSPECT

Why don't we prospect? We all know we should prospect. So, why don't we? Do you know what you need to do to succeed in real estate? If we did what we knew we should do, we'd be good. Here are a few reasons why we don't.

Procrastination

> *"Procrastination is living yesterday, avoiding today, thus ruining tomorrow."*
> —Tom Hopkins

We find more important things to do, like go to lunch, have a coffee, and commiserate with other agents who aren't producing. We tell ourselves there are more important things to do than go out and talk to people who can sign listings and purchase agreements. You know what you do to waste time.

List the three biggest time wasters in your life or business. Here are some common answers:

1. Social media consumption.
2. Talking, listening, and spending time with people who are wasting your time, their time, and their life (the zombies of the world).
3. Consuming too much television and news.

Just think about what your attitude and life would look like if you cut these in half or removed them altogether.

Let me give you a time management strategy test. It's called chunking or compartmentalizing. You want to schedule your time in 30-minute increments every day with buyers and sellers. Every 30, every 30, every 30.

You should never procrastinate meeting face-to-face with a buyer, potential buyer, seller, or potential seller EVER. You simply stick to this plan, and you will close more than others. Nothing is more important than getting your Appointments up in the CACC Formula. You can procrastinate on the rest, but ink time...NO WAY! Ink time is what I call being face-to-face with a customer who can put ink on a listing or purchase agreement. You need a minimum of one per day!

Fear

> *"Successful salespeople do things unsuccessful salespeople are afraid to do every day."*
> —Tom Hopkins

Are you afraid to talk to people? I understand the fear of rejection but don't come from your fear. Understand the market. Let's think about it. 1350 contacts. We're going to do 20; how many deals are you going to do? 1350 minus 27, what's that? 1323. What's 125,000 divided by that number? 94 dollars. If you call 1350 people, every time somebody says no, you're making 94 dollars. Every time I hear no, I'm going to get 94 bucks. Now, going back to my earlier question, if I asked you, "Do you want to come work for me? Every no you get, I'm going to hand you 94 dollars cash."

You can do it all day long. Do what I'm telling you and then say to yourself, "Thanks for the 94 dollars." I can make a contact in five minutes. How many people are making 94 bucks every five minutes? Hello! Let's go do this. Let's talk to people.

Attitude

You feel what you focus on. If you have a bad attitude, if you're not having fun, if prospecting is not fun, this is what you're focusing on. See, it's the story you tell yourself about prospecting or generating new business. Think about all the bullshit stories that are not true that you tell yourself about the most coveted occupation in the world...SALES! I love to prospect, so do you; you just haven't talked yourself into it yet!

Remember what you learned in Part 1: you have to change your paradigm. You have to be ready to regenerate and recondition your thoughts about prospecting. All this negative stuff has to go away. We've got to be new in the business and have fun. Be like a kindergartener. "Hi, my name is Sally, what's your name?" Do you ever do that anymore? Go to a kindergarten. Kids are running up and introducing themselves to everyone. It's okay to be like that. People go, "Wow, that's refreshing."

Maybe you feel like you are not that good at it, so you are embarrassed. Well, do you know how to get really good at prospecting? Repetition is the mother of learning. Everybody can prospect. Everybody can make 1350 contacts. We can all do it, but what you will do is up to you.

I'll tell you what is embarrassing, not being able to pay your bills, not being able to treat your loved ones to a meal, and not living up to your God-given potential. That is the MOST embarrassing!

What Will Happen If I Don't Prospect?

We all know what we can and should do, but we don't do it. How did I get to the top of our chain? I did the things nobody else would do every single day. Every top producer that you're around is doing it. That means they're probably working after hours, working weekends, and making sacrifices with their families. I get it. Real estate may not be conducive to awesome family life. However, it can be. If you prospect and have steady business, you can ultimately spend more time with your family.

If you are broke and starving, have no food, and have an office bill that you can't pay, you need to get out of balance and start prospecting.

When you look around your office and see your top producers, what are they doing that you're not doing? "Okay, I know what I should do. I know what I can do, but I know I'm not doing it." We've got to get leverage.

In the *SOS Playbook*, I want you to write down what will occur if you do not follow through with a prospecting plan. This is going to be a little negative, and it's going to be hard. If you don't prospect next year, what will happen in your career? Think of the worst things that could happen if you do not prospect.

Three Ways to Hone Your Prospecting Mentality

To get leverage, you need to understand what will occur if you do not take action. Here are some solutions on how to get a prospecting mentality.

- **Get an accountability partner.** Find somebody in your office that you like. It might be better to get an accountability partner that you do not like. Here's what happens when two people who like each other are accountability partners. "You didn't do it? I didn't do it either. You know what, it's totally cool. We'll just not do it." Then you will check in tomorrow. "I didn't do it again. You didn't either? That's okay." Maybe find somebody that you don't like and make him your accountability partner.
- **Spend all your money.** It will help you become very, very focused on prospecting. Now, if you're married, don't do this without your partner's consent. Go out, look at your bank account, and literally spend every dime you have. That will get you motivated, which will get you out talking to people.
- **Shop for things you can't afford.** I used to love to do this, whether it be cars, homes, vacation homes. There is stuff that you cannot afford. Look at all the cool things you wish you could afford. Tell people you love, "If I worked harder, your life could be so much better than it is now." They will be happy to keep you out there working!

Understanding Negotiations

Who do we negotiate with? Everybody. Mostly, we negotiate with ourselves. The most important negotiation you need to understand is the negotiation with yourself. Have you negotiated total mediocrity in your life and career because you're an excellent negotiator when it comes to limiting your success? I will walk you through how and why we negotiate.

- The need to avoid pain is **biological**, it is a survival instinct. When we talk about prospecting, that brings up pain for most people. Understand that when we decide we don't want to do things, especially prospect, we are trying to avoid pain.
- Whatever pain is more intense determines your actions and behavior: the pain of doing something or not doing it.
- Pain and pleasure are done through **linking** or **association**. What are you linking pain and pleasure to in your career? When we look at prospecting buyers, I link pain to buyers. I love buyers. I worked with them for 25 years, but I'm not working with them anymore. It's too painful for me. What are you linking to pain? What is so painful that you're not doing it? Why aren't you doing what you know you should do, whether it's social media-wise or whether it's calling by owners and expireds? You will do more to avoid pain and acquire pleasure, absolutely, all the time.
- The same thing that may be **painful** to one is a **pleasure** to another. Buyers may be a pleasure, or buyers may be a pain.
- We must control what we link to pain and pleasure, so we don't live our lives in a state of **reaction**. Prospecting is too painful, so I'm not prospecting. I'm just reacting to it. Buyers are too painful. If I get a buyer lead, I'm not going to do the buyer lead. I'm reacting to the leads coming in negatively.
- We will do more to **avoid** pain than to **acquire** pleasure. We gravitate toward avoiding pain. With this pain and pleasure concept, our driving forces are two things. We do things to avoid pain and create pleasure. Too painful? I'll skip it. I'm going

to do pleasure. Prospecting is too painful. What do you link to pain and pleasure?
- Breakthroughs occur at your **threshold**. Your breakthrough will happen when you say, "I am not going to take this anymore. I'm done! I need to prospect!"
- Most people don't succeed until they have enough **pain** in their life. I don't know if you're in pain or not, but we do everything to avoid pain. Is there pain in my career? Is my career totally pleasurable? What in your business right now causes you pain? There's a whole myriad of challenges we have in real estate where we say, "That's kind of painful." So, what do we do? We avoid it. We don't deal with it. Do you have a listing that you know needs a price reduction? You're like, "I know I should probably tell my client that." But you don't. Too much pain.

How to Get Leverage

People say, "Glenn, how are you so bold with buyers and sellers? How are you able to say what you say to buyers and sellers?" If I lie, if I'm passive, and if I choose not to communicate, it's too painful for me. In my head, it's too painful. I can't be in relationships with buyers and sellers where I can't say, "Guys, this is what we need to do if you're not where you want to be."

I think it's important that you link and associate what you have missed out on because of your inaction. We need to link **not** taking action to **pain**. Here's the mentality: If I don't prospect, I'm going to be in major pain. We avoid stuff because we're in pain. However, not doing things really creates the ultimate pain.

I was broke and fighting my way up in real estate. Every

time I drove by an FSBO sign, I felt pain. I had to call on it. Not calling on the FSBO caused me pain. So many of us will drive right by that by owner sign and go, "Calling on it's too painful, I'm not calling them." Or we will get the expired sheet in the office and go, "I'm not calling them, it's too painful." You need to change that to it is too painful for you to drive by when you see an FSBO sign, a garage sale sign, or any sign where somebody's saying, "Hey, any REALTOR that's smart, come and talk to me!" Did you drive by an FSBO in the past week and not go up to the door and knock on it? Every FSBO that you drive by, you're going to have to stop that car and make contact, or you're going to feel like a total failure. I can't imagine how in the world, when your livelihood and your bank account depend on you closing homes, you can just drive by an FSBO sign. Focus on what will happen if we do **not** take **action**.

Stop procrastinating. Now you control your career, instead of your career controlling you. If you wait for business to come to you, you do not control your career. If you're waiting on business to come to you, you have to do business with people who are calling you.

In the *SOS Playbook*, list three things you tend to procrastinate on in your career.

Here are some examples:

1. Developing and marketing your social media business pages.
2. Getting your past clients and sphere in a CRM so you can reach out weekly.
3. Creating LIVE social media content.
4. Personally contacting or interviewing your past clients.
5. LIVE interviews of hyperlocal businesses.
6. Getting testimonials from past clients.
7. Contacting 1 FSBO per day.

SOURCE OF SALES (SOS)

8. Creating alliances with vendors who can support and pay for marketing initiatives.
9. Showing buyers or previewing homes DAILY.
10. Listening and signing up for Source of Sales Online and LIVE events.

I did this exercise and made $100,000, simply because I identified what I was procrastinating. I committed to taking massive action. I did it. It made me money! Now is the time for you to do this and get into the high life.

Give value. Have the public say to you, "Wow, I want to do business." Then you are in control. Do you control your clients, or do they control you? What will the ultimate price be if you don't follow through? The ultimate price is that you're going to be depressed and out of this business. If you let your real estate business constantly dictate to you when you get up, go to sleep, have appointments, and don't control your business, this business will eat you up and spit you out.

Where Does Your Business Come From?

1. **FSBO**: For Sale By Owners (Fastest Source of Business Opportunity) Call one a day, minimum.
2. **Open Houses**: Three out of every 4 Sundays. One Virtual. Go LIVE every time.
3. **Expireds**: They already signed once. Call one a day, minimum.
4. **Incoming Listing and Sign Calls**: Be ready with the right attitude to convert always.
5. **Farming**: Old concept still works. Geographic, Professional, Social Media
6. **Listing Signs**: Your best Source of Business, Go get em'.

7. **Networking Club**: You need to be a member of at least one. Give more than you get.
8. **Past Clients**: The most undervalued lead source in RE. Get a plan, process, and execute for your past clients. Monthly Mailings, quarterly phone check-ins, email monthly, and one personal visit or event.
9. **Sphere of Influence**: Do they Like You, Trust You, and Refer You? If not, they are not in your sphere.
10. **Mailers**: 200 on every new listing and closing, period!
11. **Social Media**: Do you have a professional page, hyperlocal page, and go LIVE?
12. **Website**: Can people search by address, tied to Google, for your Business?
13. **Chamber Events**: Give and help others' businesses succeed, and they will help yours.
14. **Family**: Can be tough, but it is low-hanging fruit.
15. **Obituaries**: A bit gloomy, but the reality is that families need you to settle their estates.
16. **Wedding Announcements**: This is more positive and fun. High percentages of newlyweds are buying homes. Network with those people who help them!
17. **Divorce Attorneys**: Many agents have thrived in this market. Multiple deals await! Sell theirs and help them both buy a new one.
18. **Retirement Communities**: Helping seniors on their next stage of life is a win-win. Create groups, support trees, and give information on how to do this to the seniors in your life and community.
19. **Builders**: Loaded with leads, but you need to give before you get. Give them a contract to build, find

them ground, make them money, and it will all come back to you.
20. **Apartment Managers**: They have the most leads available as they know the expiration dates of the tenants. It is also helpful to host events at their properties.
21. **Business Announcements in the News**: Take note of who is moving and shaking in your community, congratulate them, and see if they also want to step up their housing game!

There are plenty of opportunities. When it's all said and done, these 21 things have a common denominator on how to get business. What's the common denominator? You! You are the common denominator. Generating leads and prospecting are worthless unless you can convert, which is what we are focusing on in the next chapter.

5

CONNECT & CONVERT

Two of my favorite words in the language of real estate training! It is time to ask yourself what your connection and conversion strategy is. This chapter will help you clarify and strategize on this question. In short, connection is similar to contacts, but it also infers a deeper bond and relationship. Once a contact is made, how fast and good are you at connecting and turning that contact into a connection? Can you feel it when that happens? Certainly, we all can. Your challenge through SOS is to make those connections in less time, in fewer words, and create them by putting your customer at ease and giving them certainty and confidence in you.

The ultimate sign you are connecting is when you can convert that connection into a signed purchase or listing agreement. Your conversion or lack thereof will be a clear indicator of whether your connection is real from the start.

I can promise you this—You will never convert unless you connect first. If you are not converting, you need to work on your connection strategies, approaches, questions, and dialogues.

Are You Ready to Convert?

Where does your business come from? Expireds, listings, networking clubs, past clients, mailers, social media, obituaries, wedding announcements, divorces; the list goes on and on. This prospecting thing isn't that hard. There are a million ways to get business. What's the common denominator? You! There are dozens of leads, but you need to know what to do with them to truly make a connection. Generating leads and prospecting are worthless unless you can connect and convert. You can get in front of people, but if you're no good as a salesperson, you will not convert.

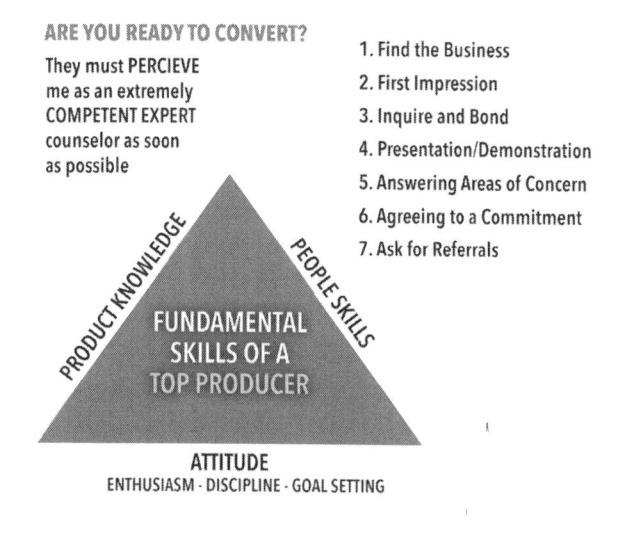

ARE YOU READY TO CONVERT?
They must PERCIEVE me as an extremely COMPETENT EXPERT counselor as soon as possible

1. Find the Business
2. First Impression
3. Inquire and Bond
4. Presentation/Demonstration
5. Answering Areas of Concern
6. Agreeing to a Commitment
7. Ask for Referrals

FUNDAMENTAL SKILLS OF A TOP PRODUCER
PRODUCT KNOWLEDGE · PEOPLE SKILLS

ATTITUDE
ENTHUSIASM · DISCIPLINE · GOAL SETTING

The 7 Steps to Professional Sales

1. **Find the Business.** You have to be able to find the business. Every person you meet is a potential customer or can lead you to a potential customer; all you need to do is ask!

2. **First Impression.** You have to be able to give an

excellent first impression. What do you do to make a good first impression? Do you have the stats? Do you have the knowledge to be the expert, so people trust you? You need to create a great strategy for first impressions. Here is mine:

1. Look great, dress for success.
2. Be interested, not interesting.
3. Have five questions ready to go that allow the prospect to talk about themselves and what they need.
4. Offer to help and serve without expecting anything back.

3. **Inquire and Bond.** Ask them questions. The power of engagement. What is the goal for a great salesperson who asks great questions? What is your customer going to say when they leave you? Find common ground. Great salespeople can do this within the first three questions. If you can't, then keep improving your skills.

4. **Presentation and Demonstration.** Do you have a good listing presentation? How are you at demonstrating property? Good presentations and good demonstrations are everything. They cut time. The key to market dominance is the ability to meet a customer, shake their hand, and get to a closing in the quickest amount of time possible. I set the expectation upfront, "Mr. and Mrs. Buyer or Seller, in a perfect world, I think I'm going to be able to have you sold and moved in the next 60 days. How does that sound to you?" I like to set time frames with buyers and sellers. "If I can get your home sold and get you another one in 60 days, are we good?"

5. **Answering Areas of Concern.** That's handling the objections. You are going to learn more about objection handling in the next part of the book.

6. **Agreeing to a Commitment.** Commitments are the key to becoming someone's agent. Start with minor agreements. May I call you to...

   1. Follow up?
   2. Email you information?
   3. Show you some other opportunities?
   4. Demonstrate market analysis and net proceeds?
   5. List your property or sell you a home?

7. **Earning Referrals.** How often should you ask for a referral? Never. You should be earning referrals. How do you feel when somebody asks you for a referral? A financial planner calls you and says, "Hey, can you give me the name of your ten most trusted friends, so I can call them and ask them if they'll do business with me?" Would you feel okay doing that? Probably not. That's asking for referrals. Next, I'm going to give you a way to earn referrals.

How to Earn Referrals

These questions will make you money if you simply ask them:

1. **"Who do you currently refer your friends, family, and business associates to in a real estate transaction?"** If you're at a party or an open house, I want to know when I meet people who they refer business to. I'm in a group of REALTORs, so this is always tougher. Before you got into real estate, did you have a REALTOR that you would refer? "I'm curious, do you refer real estate people to anybody?" You'd be amazed. Open houses are the best ones. "You know what, we really don't. I don't even know REALTORs."
2. **"Do you know anybody who needs to buy**

or sell now or in the near future?"** If you're doing your 1350, it's still going to pay you, when it's all said and done. You want to get them thinking about the time frame. As you're engaging in conversation with your referral sources, you want them to be thinking. This will help bring a name up.
3. **"Are you happy where you are now?"** This is a killer question, and it's a little bit manipulative. How many people are happy where they are now? It's a very, very good question to ask when you're out with your friends.
4. **"Would you refer yourself to you?"** This is a question to ask yourself. I hope you would refer to yourself, especially after you've done your Self Mastery.
5. **"Why would you refer someone?"** Great customer service. They are honest, and they have integrity and knowledge. Let me tell you the number one reason people refer you: They like you. Be likable.
6. **"Who was the best salesperson you ever had?"** If you have a name, write it down. Take them out to lunch and say, "You know what, you're the best salesperson I've ever had. I want to ask you, how do you do what you do?" Get their ideas.

Referral = RISK

Many people don't understand why they are not getting referrals. The reason is that referrals are too risky. If you're not getting referrals, you're too risky to give referrals to. I don't refer people who are going to make me look bad.

You're not going to refer an insurance or mortgage person if they're too risky. Trust me, if you're sloppy, if you're not committed, your friends, family, and business associates are not going to refer you. It's too risky. If you're not a pro, they will not refer you.

Defining Your Sphere

Who will you work with, and who won't you work with? **You want to work with someone who likes you.** How do you know if somebody likes you? In most cases, the way you feel about somebody is the way they feel about you. The ones that don't like me, I feel the same way about them. I hear people complain about their relationships with buyers and their sellers. "I just don't really like these people that I'm working with." I'm like, "Guess what? They don't like you either."

Only put people in your Sphere of Influence you like. Only do business with people you like. It will make this business a lot better. Do you work with a buyer or seller you don't really like? Fire them and move on.

Put people in your Sphere of Influence who trust you. Buyers trust you if they let you write full price offers for them. Buyers trust you if they take your advice on pricing. Sellers trust you if they don't overprice their listings. Sellers trust you if they list at a full commission.

If you're showing forty homes to a buyer and writing five offers before one's accepted, you have a trust problem. They don't trust you. That's hard for agents to hear, but that's the deal. Don't work with people who don't trust you because they probably don't like you either.

Investors know everything. Investors play ball in my game. I don't play ball in their game. If you're representing investors who are running you around ragged and writing terrible offers, stop that business model. Just stop it. Be done with it. They don't trust you because they think they know it all. It's better to work with people who like and trust you and do what you say.

Put people in your Sphere of Influence who will refer you. The bottom line is, if somebody has an aversion to referring me, then that's an issue. I want to make sure that they consider me a referral partner. How do you get them to refer you? When you meet with buyers and sellers, one of the most powerful things you can do is ask them about their business. Give them a few great ideas on how you can help them build their business. Then they feel like there's a partnership there.

Real estate agents often come across like this: "Hi, I'm here for a listing. I'm here to get. I'm not here to give you anything, except a marketing plan and some BS about how hard I'm going to work." Take the time to understand what your sellers and buyers do for a living and come up with creative ways to add value to their business to help them become more successful.

"I'm building my business based on referrals." I'm not saying go out and ask for referrals. When we talk about 1350, you need to be telling people, "I'm building my business based on referrals, and I could use your help." When you tell people you're building your business based on referrals, what are you really telling them? I'm going to work hard for you. If I've said it once, I've said it 1,000 times. "Mr. and Mrs. Seller, this isn't about the one home that I'm listing tonight; this is about the ten transactions you're going to refer to me in the future if I do a great job." Do you think the seller values the guy who feels like ten deals are at stake for him?

You're competing in a competitive listing situation, and the other agent doesn't even mention how to help him in what business he does. The other agent doesn't even mention that his business is so important. They're going to pick you. "I build my business based on referrals" is the most effective line

I've used in 25 years. If you're not in business to build referrals, then you're not going to last.

How to Work Your Sphere

- **Postcards** - I don't care what people say, postcards work. You should be sending 200 postcards on Just Listed, Just Sold, and Open Houses on every listing and introducing your buyers to the neighborhood with their permission. Superstar Lori Davis Smith, a top producing REALTOR and broker, goes to the twenty homes nearest the buyer's new home and asks the neighbors to sign a Welcome Home Card. This is Genius!
- **10 Minute Meetings** - No one wants to set appointments, but calling your sphere and saying, "I'll be in the area doing a CMA for a neighbor and would love to pop by for ten minutes to catch up" is a highly accepted visit!
- **Your CRM (customer relationship management)** - You should be emailing your sphere monthly, sending postcards monthly, and scheduling ten-minute meetings twice per year.
- **Thank You Notes** - Annually, at a minimum, and always after a referral.
- **Other Ideas** - Brainstorm and investigate what the most successful REALTORS do with their database....and do three of them monthly!

Work your Sphere of Influence, make those connections, and start converting them into business!

6

FSBO - FASTEST SOURCE OF BUSINESS OPPORTUNITY

When you see FSBO, you might just think For Sale By Owner. Recognize that it also stands for the Fastest Source of Business Opportunity. When I started out, I was lost, broke, and young, and I had no Sphere of Influence. However, if I went into a marketplace, I could go to any city in the US and become the number one agent. I'll tell you why. For Sale By Owners. Period. End of story.

If you called one FSBO a day, what would that do for your business? The biggest problem with FSBOs is they are not represented and do not know what they are doing. They need your help. They have a sign in the yard that says, "I need your help." Knock on the door; stop driving by For Sale By Owners. It's too painful. It may be painful to knock on the door, but it's more painful not to knock on the door.

FSBO Script

When you approach an FSBO, say, "I don't want your listing." The number one thing you want from the owner is to understand their situation and get in with them so they feel like you are a partnership. Ultimately, you want them to like you, trust you, and refer you. Here are the key questions to ask when you knock on that door:

1. **"How's it going?"** This measures how they are feeling. They are letting you know if they are frustrated or fascinated.
2. **"Have you had any offers?"** They hate that question. When they say no, don't laugh at them. If you do, do it playfully, "Oh, you haven't had any offers? Geez, we've been selling homes all over this place!"
3. **"How is your traffic activity?"** They may say they have had zero. If they have had a ton of people, follow up with, "Oh, so how do you like wasting all your time with buyers that are never going to buy your home?"
4. **"Are you selling and marketing your home on your own?"** This question lets you know if they have an advocate and a name of a person you can recruit, serve, help, or take the listing from.
5. **"How are your potential buyers?"** The point is you want them to talk about the people they're engaging with. We all know that real estate is not an easy business, and there are people that come into our lives that are not necessarily sane. Figure out what's going on with the buyer.
6. **"Do you feel you are qualified?"** They will go on and on about how unqualified they are.
7. **"Do you have an agent or an expert who can review an offer if you receive one?"** Let them tell you, "My best friend's a real estate agent." What would you say to the objection? "I'm curious, is your best friend full-time or part-time?" In real estate, half of us are part-time. "Are you

SOURCE OF SALES (SOS)

looking for a full-time or a part-time agent?" That's how you spin it. Always ask.

8. **"Do you have someone to qualify or verify your buyer's qualifications or your buyer's interests?"** I'd ask that last one, and they'd go, "Really, no."

What Do I Want From the FSBO?

1. **To really understand their situation.** No FSBO cares about you or your commission. No FSBO cares about what value you can get them in what amount of time. If you do not understand their situation, you don't have a chance. Your value comes when the FSBO can feel that you can help them out of their situation, so do that first; solve their problem, desire, or issue. Then talk about price and commission.

2. **To be able to review any offers.** When an FSBO feels comfortable sharing any offer with you for your review, you are 80% of the way home. Why would they do this? You will offer a free review, and you will often be able to take the unrepresented buyer and turn them into a sale as well!

3. **To get a list of their potential buyers and traffic.** An FSBO will hand you buyer leads if you set it up right: "Do you ever hear feedback from the buyers?"
"No."
"Well, great. I want you to record every buyer's name and email, and you can send them this form for feedback, or, if you're uncomfortable doing it, I will ask it for you or send it."

"Hey, we had ten people through."
"Great, did you get any feedback from the buyers?"
"No, we really didn't."
"Did you get their name and numbers? I can drop off an info sheet. Great, I'll go call them. I'll see you after your open house. I'll get your contacts, and I'll call those buyers."

Remember, everyone who goes through an FSBO is a buyer. Owners don't want to call buyers to see what they thought about their home, so offer to do it.

That conversation goes something like this:

"Mr. and Mrs. Buyer, you looked at a For Sale By Owner on 123 Main Street.

Just curious, did you like the home?

Do you have any future interest in the home?

Are you considering purchasing the home?

What do you like most about the area?

Are you aware of the three homes in the area similar to that?

Would you like to see those?

Would Monday or Tuesday be better to see them?"

Now, you have a buyer appointment!

4. To get them in my referral base. I often would NOT get the listing, but I would create a friendship and advocacy with the FSBO. The fact remains even if you end up NOT serving these people, they still will consider referring to you if you offer enough value and don't get paid. Some of my best referral sources have become FSBOs who never hired me, felt guilty I received no payment, and have never stopped helping me grow my business. Think long-term, not short-term.

5. To let them know I do not want to work with

SOURCE OF SALES (SOS)

them. Another reason to call By Owners is not that you want their listing, but because you'd like to make them a customer for life. "I don't want your listing. I'd like to review any offers you have at no fee. I'm not representing you, but I'd like to review them. I also want a list of your traffic. I want to contact those buyers. Would you mind if I take a look at your home? I hope you sell your home on your own. I think that would be awesome! By the way, where are you going after you sell? Do you need an agent to help you buy?"

6. **To get motivated by knowing I'm actually working.** When you call on FSBOs, you will become more motivated. You will be in the market. You will be testing your knowledge. You will actually be a real estate agent.

7. **To increase my product knowledge.** The number one source for being in sales is to know your product.

8. **To jumpstart start my business.** If you're dead in the water right now, you have no business, go call on a bunch of FSBOs. You'll be surprised at what happens to your business, attitude, motivation, and enthusiasm.

9. **To sell their home to one of my buyers or investors.** Ultimately, you want to sell the house to one of your investors. It could be that there's a home that's underpriced as an FSBO. They don't know what they're doing. One in eighty FSBOs that I used to call was grossly underpriced. I could put a deal together with a full fee. It was a great buy. It was usually a kid that inherited the home that needed to dump it.

10. **To list their home within six weeks or less.** Many times, I had an FSBO call me weeks after my first contact and follow-ups. I had written them off, but you know what, they came back and asked me to list the property. I found out that six weeks is usually the threshold for FSBOs before they list.

The Greatest Question to Ask an FSBO

"What will you do if it doesn't sell?" They hate that question. Make sure you're asking people that.

THE FSBO PROCESS

There's a fortune to be made communicating with FSBOs. Let's review the process:

1. Find out where they are.
2. Decide if you can work with them.
3. Do a CMA and net proceeds sheet.
4. Deliver a listing presentation.
5. List the property.
6. Give them great service and earn referrals!

Do not pass up on FSBOs. If you use the questions and strategies within this chapter, you will soon recognize that FSBO stands for Fastest Source of Business Opportunity!

7

THE OPEN HOUSE

I've been in real estate long enough to know some agents love and believe in the open house and those who don't. I will say this first: no matter your opinion of an open house, you will be correct. I have seen agents use open houses to build their careers!

I specifically know of a million-dollar commission salesperson who came to a new market, sat in luxury open houses, cultivated and developed their client base, locked down the highest priced subdivision in the market, and has never looked back! Guess what, you can too!

Five Great Reasons to Hold an Open House:

1. If an offer has been or is about to be placed, it puts the seller in a great position of leverage, a position they will thank you for and remember when it comes time to refer you. It also has proven to get a deal signed so the open house won't proceed and has procured higher values for many of my sellers.
2. It is a great lever to get price reductions from the

seller. Not only does an agent work at an open house, but a seller does. They have to clean, plan what to do, get sitters for kids, deal with the dogs, etc. Open houses show you are committed to them by using your time. If you do them the first four Sundays of the listing, the sellers will beg not to do anymore, or they will be open to reducing the price because of your efforts.
3. It is a great way to secure new clients (buyers & sellers) as many people who walk through are unhappy with their agent and are looking for an agent who works weekends. At a minimum, it gives you the ability to add to your mailing list and ask for referrals.
4. It is the best way to get a double commission and practice limited agency. Trust me, your odds of representing both buyer and seller go up dramatically if you sit in your listing and know how to sell it.
5. It is a great time to set and plan your week during downtime. I can guarantee you if you take an hour on a Sunday to plan your week, organize your contacts, set your appointments, and visualize your week, you will be on fire every week. If you do not have four pendings, you need to be in an open house.

Be the Expert

Potential clients must perceive you as highly confident, an expert, and a counselor as soon as possible. Have you ever met some of your peers at an open house? Most of them probably don't present themselves as experts.

If somebody walked in off the street and said, "Hey, can you tell me what the low value, the high value, and the median

SOURCE OF SALES (SOS)

value lists for this neighborhood?" What would you do most of the time?

"Uh..." Right. You would not look like an expert. Be the expert.

How are you demonstrating your knowledge and expertise at your appointments with buyers and/or sellers? It's found in statistics. There are some statistics that you need to know:

- Highest price? Lowest price? Average price?
- How many homes in the area are for sale?
- How many homes sold last year?
- How many homes sold in the township?
- How many homes sold from major street to major street?
- What were the average days on market?

That's expertise, versus going "I don't have any idea at all, um, I don't know, how about I just cut my fee, and we list?"

You want to be that agent who says, "Welcome to our open house. I'm curious, do you live in the neighborhood? Are you aware of the highest and lowest values sold in this area? Would you be interested in knowing that? Are you aware of how many homes are for sale in this subdivision? Would you be interested in going to see those?" That sounds like somebody confident in their expertise.

The Open House

1. **Retail Real Estate Day**: Believe it or not, I make a lot of money on open houses, and I list many properties on open houses. If you work in a big company, plenty of people will do them for you if you don't want to do them. The problem is people don't

expect much from open houses. They show up and put their sign in the yard; that's it.

2. **Contact the Neighbors**: As you're sitting in your open house on Sunday, I want you to feel uneasy because you are thinking to yourself, "I could create my destiny. I could have so much money in the bank if I just talked to the neighbors." If you're in a neighborhood, and there's a real estate sign three doors down, knock on the doors around that listing.

Imagine if an agent came and knocked on your door and said, "Hi, I'm Glenn Bill with ABC Realty. I want to let you know that your neighbor's home will be open. I'm just curious, do you know anybody who wants to buy or sell in your neighborhood now or in the near future? Have you ever been in the home? I wanted to invite you in. I have some warm cookies and coffee down there. We'd love to see you." Would you go, "There's an agent that supersedes all my expectations"? I did an open house where I bought $100 in signs. I had an espresso bar and free ice cream. It cost me a couple hundred bucks. I got an $800,000 buyer out of it. The buyer had never seen any agent do that.

3. **Post on Social Media**: Invite your sphere and theirs. You never know whom they know who might need that house or want to move into that area. Not to mention, it is a great way to see them in person, and it makes you look successful.

4. **In-Person Is Bes**t: You are in sales, get used to it; nothing beats belly-to-belly!

SOURCE OF SALES (SOS)

5. **Get Visitors to Sign In** (with accurate information): You can check on Google or Facebook immediately to confirm. "Mr. and Mrs. Buyer, we always like to know if our marketing of the open house is working. We're hoping you will sign in and share with us how you found this open house. It really helps us to get your address and email so we can source where the best neighborhood is to market this property!"

6. **Five Great Questions for Visitors**:

   - Are you from the area?
   - Are you aware of the highest priced home in the area?
   - Are you aware of the lowest priced home in the area?
   - Are you aware of how many homes are for sale in the area?
   - What is the greatest asset to this area for you?

7. **The Three Options that May Work**: You should have a home that is less money, more money, and the best value on your fingertips to talk to them about if the home they are in does not work.

8. **Know the Most Important Amenities**: Nothing is worse than when an open house client hits the door, and you have no information about the bedrooms, baths, fireplaces, garages, lot size, etc. Trust me, it happens, even to the best of us when we don't prepare!

9. **Show Up with an ABS Mindset**: Attitude-Based Selling plays a huge role in your success with open

houses. An Attitude-Based Mindset encourages enthusiasm, discipline, and goal setting. How many people do open houses and don't have any of those three? What is your enthusiasm level? Are you genuinely excited to be there? Are you slumped on a couch, or do you have music going and cookies in the oven? Are you full of a contagious vitality that people want to engage with?

When it comes to open houses, how disciplined are you? Have you contacted the neighbors, posted on social media, done a LIVE video, have flyers set and accurate? Do you have a disciplined plan to take on an open house program? Are you setting open house goals? How many mailers, how many posts, how many neighbors hit, how many signs, how many visitors, how many follow-ups, how many people will you ask for referrals, how many conversions will you get?

Prospecting Around Current Listings

1. Ask a **big** listing producer. If a fellow agent came up to me and said, "Glenn, would you mind if I called everyone in the neighborhood that you're marketing in?" I would let them.
2. If you get a listing on a street, there is an 80% chance one of the neighbors within **twenty houses** will be listing within the next six months. Twenty owners to the left, twenty owners to the right, and forty owners across the street; those are pretty good odds. Wouldn't it drive you crazy until you figured out which one?
3. Open houses are the best time to prospect. How many people knock on doors and say, "May I put a

sign in your yard?" Do you know how much people appreciate that? Why don't we do it? Too painful. You don't want to interrupt them, and you don't want to do it over and over again, but at least one time, it would be good.

Phraseology

"We are so excited to represent Mr. and Mrs. Seller on the sale of their home down the street. Would you happen to know if you or somebody would like to upgrade their home in the neighborhood? Are you familiar with the house? Would you like to view the home?"

What can you do at open houses that could change your paradigm right now? We all waste time with open houses. Stop wasting time; get creative. What's the one thing you can do at your open houses that nobody else does?

Prospecting Mastery
SOS Challenge

To start applying the CACC Formula and Active Prospecting strategies to your life and work, complete the exercises in the *SOS Playbook*. If you don't already have your *SOS Playbook*, visit www.glennbill.com/sosplaybook to download your copy.

PART III

SELLER MASTERY

The fear that REALTORS have when it comes to sellers has always amazed me. When I ask agents if they would rather have a buyer or seller, about 80% say a buyer, especially new ones. Why the fear?

Sellers offer more in return to an agent. They guarantee you a paycheck, but you cannot be a pretender when dealing with them. We will talk about buyer skills in the next part of the book. Still, the reality is showing buyers, opening doors, and being a professional tour guide is a great way to pretend you are a productive, profitable REALTOR. It's easy, but it's NOT a good use of your time and not a profitable way to structure your business.

When you harness the power of what I will teach you in the following pages, it will let you dictate your career instead of having your career dictate you. It will allow you to plan your paychecks, build your bank account, and create certainty in your business and life. Here is the catch: only the few who master the seller, train themselves, read this book, and master my teachings will reap the real estate sales game rewards.

There is only one way to do the units, control the market, and not depend on lead gen and other shiny objects to get you to riches in the real estate brokerage business. It is Mastering the Seller.

My goal for you is simple: You stand out when you walk into a listing appointment. You are different than the rest, you become irresistible to a seller, and they LISTEN and DO what you tell them in terms of price, commission rate, timing, and all other negotiable items that occur during the process of a listing contract through to closing.

Just imagine how great your life and career would be if all you did was take listings that sell in 30 days and close in 60? You are already getting more relaxed.

Want to know how to create this type of life? KEEP READING!

8

ENGAGEMENT QUESTIONS

"If I say it, they tend to doubt it. If they say it, it's true."
—Tom Hopkins

The key to any interaction with buyers or sellers is this: ask questions. One of the greatest real estate agents I know, my former partner Tim O'Connor, would always ask questions. A conversation with Tim was fascinating because he would simply ask question after question after question.

Seller Mastery is very much about your questioning process. At the listing table, you need to be asking engagement questions. When I find agents who don't like to list or are not successful at listing, I find agents who don't have the proper questioning process.

Why You Need to Master the Art of Questioning

How do we get everybody to say what we want them to say? Through mastering the art of questioning. The best, most skilled, most profitable, wealthiest salespeople have an innate ability to ask questions. True **Seller Mastery** in this business comes from questioning. It's an art, and it's not easy. I learned a lot about questioning from Tom Hopkins in *How to Master the Art of Selling*.[1] Here's is what you need to know about mastering the art of questioning:

1. **Gain control.** Do you have control over the dialogue? Do you have the ability to lead a conversation with questions? When you're on the floor, who is in control of a conversation? How do you gain control of a conversation? Those who ask questions are in control. Do your buyers and sellers control you, or do you control your buyers and sellers?

The buyer calls in, "Hey, how much is the home? How many bedrooms?" That buyer is controlling the conversation. Ask questions in return "$225,000, is that the price range you're looking at? Four bedrooms, is that how many bedrooms you want? Are you looking for a big yard?" It's called the porcupine technique because you want to toss the questions back at them and stay in control. You're not going to allow yourself to be controlled by your customers and clients anymore.

2. **Determine what they want.** Do you know what your buyers and sellers want? Are you working with some people and going, "What do you want?!" Are you working with people, and you just have no idea? How can you find them what they want if you don't really know what they are looking for?

3. **Get minor agreements.** Proper questioning gives you minor agreements. "Mr. and Mrs. Buyer, if this home feels right to you today, would you consider purchasing it? If I come in at the right price, would you consider listing with me?" We want to build minor agreements and turn minor agreements into major agreements.

4. **Arouse and control their emotions.** Real estate is the most emotional sale in the marketplace. Questions arouse the emotions of our buyers and sellers. I don't mind an emotional buyer and seller because emotion creates motion. I want people, once they're emotional, to act. It is no good if they're passive when you're showing them homes. "I'm not really emotionally invested in this. I don't have to own. I don't have to buy." Yes, you do have to buy! I'm not working with you if you don't have to buy. I'm going to refer you to somebody else, and you're going to waste their time.

5. **Isolate areas of concern.** People have legitimate concerns, and we must be able to isolate those. Salespeople's biggest mistakes are that they don't necessarily drill down to find out the biggest concern. "What's your biggest concern about listing with me?" Questioning will help you with that.

6. **Acknowledge or confirm a fact.** "Mr. Seller, now that you've seen my marketing plan, do you feel confident that I can get the job done?" Let's confirm that fact, so everyone agrees.

7. **Help them rationalize their decision.** So many times, you just need to push sellers. "Do you really think I should reduce the price?" Yes. If you want a $10,000 reduction, how much of a reduction should you tell them you want? 20,000, but he can settle at 10.

All the time, people want certainty in their life. You must tell your buyers and sellers, "I really think you're making the right decision here," especially, when they've cut their price. Do you say that to your clients and customers? There can be a lot of animosity; you must help them feel good and help them rationalize.

The Power of Engagement Questions

You want to ask questions that make clients face reality. What you know or don't know, depending on your experience, and what they know or don't know, depending on their experience, may or may not be reality.

Reality is simply found in these three questions:

1. Do you want the actual price or one that makes you feel great?
2. Do you want to keep the home if it does not sell?
3. Are you on a time frame to move?

These three questions will bring their reality to the table.

You want to ask questions that are tough to ask. Take the risk. The riskier questions you ask a seller, the more you will earn respect. "What happens if you don't sell? What happens if you don't move? How upset is your spouse going to be if you screw this up and don't do what I say?" Those are risky questions.

You want to ask questions that produce direction and finality. I don't want to engage a buyer or a seller unless we have a direction and a finality. It's called starting with the end in mind. When you meet your customer, start with the end in mind. Let's stop working with open-ended people, where there's no direction or end in mind. We're going to meet them, ask engaging questions, put a time frame on this thing, and they're going to go, "Hey, this is a nice little package this real estate agent has given me."

We're not going to work with people who go, "If we sell, we sell. It doesn't matter. I like spending time with you because you're awesome."

Why Do We Ask Engaging Questions?

They save you time. I am not interested in wasting time. If you're talking to 1,350 people a year about real estate, you can tell your time wasters, "You know what, unfortunately, I'm busy working with people that are on a time frame." Stop wasting your time and stop working with people who are time wasters.

They let people know where you stand. Do you let your customers know where you stand? Or do they bully you and push you around?

They can earn you respect. Are you being respected by your clients or customers? I've been disrespected. It doesn't work, and it's not a good way to do business.

When Do We Ask Engagement Questions?

Ask engagement questions:

- After they have vented.
- After you have reached a timeframe.
- During the initial interview.

How Do We Ask Them?

1. You need to ask engagement questions with sincerity. Don't shove it in their face.
2. You must be sincere when asking engagement questions without making them wrong. Give them a **choice**. Many people lose listing presentations because they're going in trying to be right instead of letting the seller be right. Your sellers are wrong when it comes to pricing. Maybe 1 out of 10 sellers hits the price on the head. When I ask the magic

question, "So, what do you think your home is worth?" 9 out of 10 times, they are wrong. Don't make them wrong; give them the evidence to show them the right number.
3. Involve the future. If you get prospects thinking in the future, it motivates them to look for solutions. YOU are their solution. People are motivated by what can be, not what is.
4. Make it about getting the lowest or highest price. We know this for a fact: 80% of the prospects on the planet make getting the most money as a seller and the lowest price as a buyer a priority. Of course, when that is established, you become the answer to making that happen, only if they listen to you and follow your SOS advice!

Turn Frustration into Fascination

> *"Learn how to turn frustration into fascination."*
> —Jim Rohn

Do you ever feel frustrated? Maybe you are frustrated with your sellers because they won't reduce their price, they want you to hold open houses, and they want you to do brokers' open houses. Instead of saying, "My buyers won't buy. They're taking my weekends and driving me crazy," look at your seller and go, "You're so fascinating." Don't be frustrated; be fascinated with them.

Let Them Vent

Sellers are very, very proud of their home. Sit in, ask a few engagement questions, and let them go on, and on, and on, and on. "We redid this, we redid that. I put a new deck on; I did that deck myself. I painted the whole thing myself," and you're like, "Oh wow, you picked that color." It's going to be tough; I understand. They need to vent. Do not go and puke on a seller during your listing presentation by talking too much. Your goal in your listing presentation is to let them talk it all out.

What they're saying will be wrong 90% of the time. What they're saying is going to fascinate you. "Mr. Seller, that is so fascinating. You overpaid for your property. Ooh, this is going to be a tough one." You've got to let them vent. The more they talk upfront, the better.

Avoid the temptation to interrupt, critique, or argue. You are not going to tell them they are wrong. You're going to let them vent. That's how you build trust. If you don't let them vent all the wrong information and misinformation they believe, they're never going to think you listened to them.

Some people are argumentative in this business, and some people interrupt. What do we need to do when we're with the seller? We need to let them vent.

Understand you're going to get frustrated. They're going to say, "Well, this home should sell right away, and it should sell for $50,000 more. Look at the improvements that we did." You're just going to sit there and look at them, thinking, "You are so wrong, but I'm going to be fascinated and keep my mouth shut." Let them vent - a key listening tool. The more you listen, the more they're going to feel you care.

Stay Positive and Show Gratitude

Mention why you like working in real estate with them. Okay, this is hokey, but hokey works. "Mr. and Mrs. Buyer/Seller, I want to let you know I really enjoy working with you because you are so upbeat, trusting, always on time, and you take such great care of your home."

At open houses, highest loyalty rate, sellers love when you

leave a personal note after the open house and thank them. Do you do that? "Dear Mr. and Mrs. Buyer/Seller, thank you for leaving your home in such a great condition. You did an awesome job preparing the house. I can't thank you enough." That builds trust. Avoid the call at 9 p.m., "Hey, we had an open house, got any feedback for me? Anything?" They don't trust you if you don't give them feedback after an open house. It is easier to write a note than deal with their questions at 9 o'clock when you get the call.

The Best Way to Listen

Write it down. When I was 20 and listing homes like crazy, I did this naturally. I made it a point to write down everything a seller told me, even if it was wrong. Write it down, and then you can write WRONG next to it, but don't let them see that!

The best way to listen is to write things down. That's also how they know they're being heard. If you have a great attitude, and you have a lot of energy, and you write everything down - you're halfway there. You let them vent - you are getting closer to a listing.

9

SETTING THE TABLE WITH SELLERS

"Success is buried on the other side of frustration."
—Tony Robbins

Some sellers are smart and understand the game. We don't need to sit down and give them an hour and a half presentation on value. If they've got the value, then move on. You don't need to show how smart you are if they're ready to go at that number.

Understand that all sellers want the highest price. How can you attract sellers that really want to sell quickly? I want highly motivated sellers calling me asking me to sell their homes. Doesn't everybody want that? Can you imagine four or five people calling a month going, "I'm highly motivated, and I'm ready to price it right. I need to sell my home."? That's happening with me. I'm going to show you how to do it.

The Set-Up

I call this "setting the table." When setting the table, here are some questions that I like to ask first:

- **"How much do you want for your property?"** You're not saying this is how much you can get them; you just want to know how much they want. Sometimes they'll say, "Well, I don't want to tell you. You tell me." What would you say to that? "Well, after I show you the information, are you willing to list at the price I suggest?" Engaging question. "Are you prepared to look at the information I'm giving you regarding value if it seems reasonable and fair to you? Would you consider listing at that price today?" Those are engaging questions. That's what you need to be saying.
- **"What happens if you can't get that price?"** It's an unbelievable listing question for them. "Ooh, I've never had an agent ask me that question before. Well, I don't know. I guess I'd sell it for less." If they reply, "I won't sell," don't list it if that's their attitude.
- **"Have you ever sold a home before?"** If they say yes, let them vent and explain their story. Let them tell you how good or bad their experience was. Sometimes, they'll say it was great. Then you keep asking questions.

"What was so great?"
"Well, we sold it in a day."
"Why do you think it sold in a day?"
"Well, we put it at a really good price."
"Fabulous. Do you think we should put it at a really good price again?"
"Yeah." Good, my listing presentation is not going to be long.

Understand that sellers want the highest price! Sellers

don't want to list too low. Their biggest concern is that they are listing with a dud who will not get the home sold.

Ten Questions for Sellers

You will have so much fun with these questions. They won't even ask *you* questions when you're done asking these questions. They won't even ask you to show your marketing plan. They're going to go, "This agent understands me, and this agent gets me. This agent is somebody who asks questions I've never heard before. This agent is the one that's going to get me moved."

> 1. **"Do you feel this information is fair? Why or why not?"** We all have been there, right? "Here's your comps: 205, 208, 203, 205. Mr. and Mrs. Seller, think this is fair?"
> "No, I need two and a quarter."
> "Well, if you're a buyer, here's a great engagement question - why would you pay 15,000 more than the comps? Could you tell me that Mr. and Mrs. Buyer? Is it fair or not?" Home-sellers are very personal, and they get into this whole fairness thing. "That's not fair; my house is nicer." Even though it's not, right?

You need to get them to acknowledge if this is a fairness issue or marketability issue. Then, you need to explain that fairness has no place in the marketplace. Fair is only what a buyer will pay. Fair means nothing. I want to get it out of the way. I want them to get their emotions met, and I want them to say that it's fair when it's all said and done. If they feel like it's not fair, they're not going to trust you, they're not going to like you, and they're not going to refer you business. "Let's all agree that the information I'm presenting is going to be fair. Are you good with that?" Great place to start.

2. **"Would you rather not sell and stay where you are?"** They hate this question, especially when one spouse wants to sell more than the other. What do you think most people say when I ask this? "Nobody has ever really asked me that before." We go in and say, "We're going to list it, and we're going to sell it."

When I go to list a property, I say, "Look, one of the options is that you're going to stay here." Make them live through that; make them feel that they're going to have to stay where they are forever if we don't do business. They're going to go, "No, no, no, no, no! We don't want to stay here." Now, my listing presentation is ready to go.

3. **"Would you consider staying?"** Make them face the reality of staying there. Everybody wants to get better. They don't really want to stay in the same place.
"If you can't get my price, I'm not listing."
"Good, maybe you should consider staying."
"Well, I really don't want to."
"Good, I don't want you to either, so let's quit saying that. No, let's not consider that. Let's go ahead and move forward."

4. **"If you were the buyer, or when you are the buyer, would you want me to perform the same research?"** Buyers have buyers' agents; they're doing their research. Sellers want to fight the research. Simply put the shoe on the other foot. "When you're buying a home, should I just call the seller and say,

SOURCE OF SALES (SOS)

'Hey, how much do you need?'"... "Glenn, I really need two and a quarter." Well, buyers don't care what you need. It's going to be based on the research.

5. **"Would you pay more than market value?"** Markets are cyclical, but lately, lack of supply dictates that the home goes to the highest bidder. List price offers rarely get the house. A conversation about how much over list is imperative; you must have a strategy and a plan. My strategy is always asking this question, "How much do you want the home? At what price are you willing to lose it?" Then start asking by price: $5000 over, $10,000 over, etc. Certainly, your ability to use and negotiate escalation clauses is a key to winning offers for your client, and I strongly recommend using those as often as possible.

6. **In a perfect world, where do you see yourself in three months? Why?"** Talk to them about the future. Get them thinking that this home's terrible; they have to go. Start with the end in mind. "Three months from now? Gosh, I see myself being moved." Or "Well, I see you doing your 10th open house after not reducing the price and us getting out of our home for a 30th showing." That's probably not where they see themselves. Get them to see the future. This question forces them to move mentally.

7. **"Is the commission and price the most important consideration for you, or is the why above more important?"** You just asked them where they see themselves in three months. "Why are you moving? Is moving more important than what you get for your home and the commission you're going to

pay? I like to head commission off at the beginning." The "why" is more important.

8. **"Do you not feel I'm worth it?** That's important. It lets you know if you have a price-based priority, seller or not. This is a commission question. If they start pounding you on your fee, ask them, "Do you feel I'm not worth it?" Some ruthless, mean people will say you're not worth it. Do you like somebody that limits your work? Do you trust somebody who says you're worth nothing? Probably not a good relationship, probably not a listing you should take.

"Are you just doing business with me because I'm cheaper?" I find nothing more irritating and demeaning than being commoditized by a potential client. There are two reasons people do this. One, they do not value you. Two, you have given no value. As Gitomer says, "When you give no value, all that is left is price." If the sole reason people do business with you is that you are the cheapest, you will never make it in this business. I teach you how to develop your value in the **Value Mastery** portion of the book. However, the most important thing I can tell you is that your fee has nothing to do with whether people hire you; if it does, you are out of the game.

9. **"Has anyone else taken the time to preview your competition?"** When I go to list a property, "Mr. and Mrs. Seller, if somebody looks at your home, they're going to look at ten other homes. I'm just wondering, has any real estate agent that you've interviewed been in your ten competitor's homes? I have been. Here they are." Tell them about their

SOURCE OF SALES (SOS)

competition. Say, "By the way, when the next agent walks in, ask them about these ten homes."

Do something for the seller on behalf of the seller before the sale. What are you doing before the listing presentation? Are you bringing value to your listing? I suspect that if you go to the ten other homes that that home competes with, you're going to be a better lister, you're going to have more market knowledge, and you're going to be more valued.

I always try to do the ten homes below the expected list price. If I listed at 250, I would look at the 225 market. If there was something for 235, 240, 15 grand less than we're starting with, that's better. You better believe I'm going to pull that up on my iPad and say, "You're going to be at 250? Do you see this home? Not happening. Ask the other agent if they know about this home."

If you walk in after me, your presentation will be dead in the water. I used to cook other agents with that all the time. "Glenn, can you believe it? An agent came in here, and they didn't even preview the homes we were listing against." Here's the secret - if you go against me in a listing presentation, you better know what the competition is because I will set the seller up.

10. **"If you could close your eyes and imagine how the sale of your house would go, what would that look like?"** "Gosh, I've never been asked that before. I have no idea what it looks like." When they say they don't know, guess who gets to create and paint the picture? You do. If you have any closing skills, they're going to say, "I don't know, what

does it look like to you?" You're going to say, "Great, give me the brush and let me show you the paint. Here's how it looks like to me, you listen to what I say, you list at my price, you pay me a full fee, you let me have unfettered access to your home, you do the things I tell you to do, and we get this sold in the first week. We close in 30 days, and we will put you in your new home in the next 45 days. How does that sound to you?" That question is money in the bank. Please ask it.

Five Great Questions

1. **"If I sell your home tomorrow at full price with multiple offers, are you going to be okay with that?"** In a hot market, May and June, remember that. Multiple offers. Do you know what really pisses a seller off? Full price, multiple offers on the first day. Did you overprice it, underprice it, or hit it on the head if that happens? You hit it right on the head! "Mr. and Mrs. Seller, don't be offended if we get multiple offers on your property because you have a great home, you've done everything we've told you to do, and we're probably going to hit it right on the head if we do. The market is that good right now."

If it does happen, they're not upset with you. That's off the table now. "Ugh, they underpriced my listing." No! This is what I expect, and this is what you should expect. It's okay.

2. **"Why did you purchase this home?"**
"It was a great deal and an awesome buy."
"Well, the reason that you bought this home is

probably going to be the same reason the next buyer buys the home. If it was a great deal when you bought it, what do you think we're going to have to make your price to sell your home? A great deal."

If it was a great deal when you bought it, chances are it's going to have to be a great deal when you sell it. Whenever they tell you it was a great buy, go, "Uh oh, I didn't realize this, but something is going on with this home. Chances are you're going to have to do it too."

3. "What happens if it's not sold in 30 days? Are you going to fire me? Are you going to reduce your price? Do you want me to do three more open houses? What are we going to do?" If you're not meeting with your sellers every 30 days, you're missing the boat. If they are priced right, they sell in 30 days or less. When you commit to **Seller Mastery**, it's going to happen more for you than not when you commit to this type of conversation. You're going to become a better lister, a more profitable agent, and you're going to control your time.

4. "What are the three most important considerations that you are going to make when selling your house and hiring a REALTOR?" Do I trust them? How much time is it going to take? I want the highest price.

Guess what my presentation is going to be? It's going to be about whatever the hell they're looking for. They want somebody who is honest. I'm honest. Let me show you how honest I am. I've got video testimonials on my honesty.

5. "Do you understand what I mean when I say we're in this together? We are in this together."
I cannot tell you how important it is for you to build a relationship with your sellers. The spirit of teamwork, and this question gets it. Are you really in it together with your buyers and sellers or not?

BONUS: "Are there any more questions?"
Floyd Wickman shared the greatest closing question. When you're done with your engagement questions, when you're done with your listing presentation - always ask this: "Are there any more questions?" When they say, "No." Boom. You move on, and you list the property.

10

SELLER ATTITUDES AND PERCEPTIONS

Perception is defined as insight, intuition, knowledge gained by perceiving. We have to get through our seller's perceptions of us and the marketplace. When you walk through the door of a potential agent or a seller, what are people thinking of you? What's your image? When I go to a listing, what does a seller see when I walk in the door?

I wore a suit and tie every day. I know people who don't believe in it. That's fine. You don't have to be me. However, unfortunately, how you are initially perceived is based on how you look and appear. If I'm going to close a $20,000 fee on a listing, I'm going to look good. I will create a professional, serious relationship because I negotiate very high fees. It's not going to be casual, but it will always be friendly. Most importantly, I want to give them value.

Attitudes Your Sellers Challenge You With

- **You guys make too much money.** Just look at what agents post about their success, trips, cars, and year-end self-accolades. Maybe we should be posting about late hours and saving deals.

- **All you need to do is stick it into BLC/MLS.** Sometimes, if it's priced at 50% of the value, all you need to do is stick it in. However, before you stick it into BLC, you have to decide if you want to list it at 50% of the value. We can stick our sign in the yard, but look at all of the work you do before sticking the sign in the yard. All the preparations, all the engagement questions, all the research - going to look at the ten other properties. The perception that you make too much money is not correct. We don't just stick it in! Your value is found in your expertise, staging, marketing, negotiating, vendor referrals, and competitive analysis!

- **Your time is not important.** Sellers don't care about your time. Your time is important, just not as important as their time. SOSers know how to present and leverage time in their favor to get buyers and sellers to do what is best for all.

- **I want a kickback.** "This agent will give me a kickback or discount." I understand that there are people in your exact market who charge less. You are going to learn how to beat that. If you are a commission cutter, that will be the perception. If the word gets out on the street, he works at X%, they're going to know it. You've created your street value. You can change that tomorrow if you decide to say, "Look, I'm only doing this if I get paid right." I didn't negotiate one fee this year. Period, end of story. The perception was, "If I'm hiring Glenn, it's going to be a full boat - that guy's got value."

- **You're such a salesman.** Being a proud

salesman is a benefit to all in the transaction. We have plenty of REALTORS who aren't proud and look at their production level. Trust me, buyers and sellers don't mind a strong, confident, proud agent. The question is, are you too proud? Selling is a learned skill. Once you master the SOS techniques, you will not seem so "Salesmanny." I always took it as a compliment.
- **You're only in it for the money!** Do people question your intentions in this business? HELL YES! You need to develop the skills in this book to dispel this perception. Doing more for the client when selling their home is a great test. What have you done for their business, their family, friends, or community? We are more than just money-hungry salespeople.

Your Attitudes & Perceptions

I want you to understand how people generate their attitudes towards you. Think about your manners and how you carry yourself. When you go into a listing, don't go, "Phew, this market's tough. Not sure we can sell it." Not wanting to list with you!

Think about how you approach the sellers. What is your posture when you walk? I am so fired up when I get to go into a listing.

What's your state of mind? What are your feelings? Are you bringing certainty to a seller? You can sell any listing if it is priced right. "There's no way you can sell my listing; it has been on the market three years." Respond with, "I have an idea. How about cutting the price in half and see what happens?" Give them certainty. "I'm sure I can sell your listing. I'm just not sure I can sell your listing at the price you want. What's more important, getting your listing sold or getting the price you want? That's the deal. I can sell any home, but I can't sell it for ten grand over market value."

What are your attitudes and perceptions towards listing? I love listings. How do you do both sides of the transaction if you don't have the listing? I have an excellent attitude about listings. Guaranteed fee, chance to double-dip. How can you not love to list? Understand that if I listed 30 homes next year, at an average price of 175, I could gross close at 125 grand and not show one buyer. Amazing! I don't know what your attitude towards listing is. I'm hoping to inspire you to want to list more real estate. This is the name of the game. If you list, you last.

Attitude is a feeling or emotion towards a fact or state. Attitude is about the emotion of a seller. We're in an emotional business. The key to life is the ability to control your emotions and the emotions of people around you. How do we do that? By being an attractive person, and by understanding emotions, attitudes, and perceptions.

How do you react to these attitudes? How do you react to these perceptions? What is your reaction? "No! I'm not in for the money! You're wrong!" Don't make them wrong.

I used to get very upset and confrontational when people would ask me to reduce my fee. I would make them wrong. I was sometimes bordering on physically threatening. I don't like people messing with my fees. I don't like them messing with your fees either, but getting confrontational is not the way to react.

1. **Ask why they feel that way.** People come after us a little bit. If they're insulting you, or they have an attitude, "Oh, you're such a salesman. You make too much money." Ask them why they think you make too much money.

2. **Listen intently.** When you ask them, listen to the

answer! Why do you feel like I'm such a salesman? Care about what they say.

3. **Tell them sincerely how you feel about their attitude.** "Mr. and Mrs. Seller, I want to tell you sincerely that our company is always looking for great real estate salespeople. Since it's so easy, I think you should join our company."
"Oh, I could do real estate."
"Great, then why don't you? Sincerely, I want to know."

4. **Deal in facts, not emotion.** "Oh, you're only in it for the money!" "No, I'm not. You're a bitch!" Don't go there. Deal with facts. "Mr. and Mrs. Seller (who's assaulting me and who has a bad attitude and a bad perception,) I can tell I'm only in this to build my business based on referrals." It's not about this one home sale that we will talk about tonight. It's about the ten home sales that we're going to do in the future together over the next five years." Every transaction is worth ten if you bring value.

5. **Use questions to handle them.** Always answer a question with a question. Remember the porcupine technique where you toss questions back at them to stay in control of the conversation.

Don't let negative attitudes and perceptions bring you down. Stay focused on the goal and keep a positive attitude. You can change their misperceptions and gain clients for life.

11

THE NET SHEET - YOUR BEST TOOL

I'm a big net sheet guy. In my opinion, the strongest form you have is the net sheet form because everybody wants to know where they are. We all have emotional needs. The number one emotional need of a person in a real estate transaction, especially the seller, is the need for certainty. When it's all said and done, the sellers want certainty about two things: certainty that it's going to get sold and certainty about for how much. The more certainty you can deliver to a seller, the more apt they are to use you. Provide certainty through your net-proceed-sheet.

21 Reasons to Use a Net Proceeds Sheet

As you read these twenty-one reasons why you need to do the net sheet, remember this is really about how to service the seller.

1. **The Net Proceeds Sheet is your best friend.**

2. **It gets you listings.** If you go into a listing and

don't do a net sheet, and another agent does, you're going to lose the listing.

3. **It helps get offers accepted.** They want certainty about a few things. How much will I get, and how much will it get sold for? We have it off our notes: it's going to get sold, but to be able to tell a seller within 100 dollars is excellent. "Mr. and Mrs. Seller, I want to ask you a question, would it be better in 30 days if you had a check for 16,553 dollars or not?" Great closing question. Your net sheet will get that for you. We're putting them in the future. There's your net sheet with the number. Having 16,000 dollars in your pocket? That's the name of the game.

4. **It gets your seller focused on the right issues.** The bottom line is that possession is not an issue, inspections aren't an issue, closing costs aren't an issue. What's the issue? When do we close, and how much cash will I get? Nobody cares about anything else. Get them focused on the net. There are so many moving parts in an offer that people can get upset and crazy about it. The bottom line is, what's your number? Here's your number, everything else you don't need to worry about.

5. **There are two issues sellers must decide.** When I'm closing a seller on an offer, they must decide 1. Is it enough money and 2. Do I really want to sell? Those are the decisions. Help them with those decisions.

I do my net sheets on a worst-case scenario. Here's my language, "Mr. and Mrs. Seller, I know this seems a little bit low, but I always like to do worst-case scenarios." They might say, "Well, I want you to write it $8,000-$10,000 more." Then they make me change my suggested price. As professionals, we know what a home will sell for normally. Many agents just don't have the guts to tell the seller.

One great way to do it is with your best friend the net sheet. They go, "Well, that's not the price we wanted." Say, "Oh, I must have made a mistake. I'm sorry, but you should keep that number in mind. You're going to be seeing it in 30-60 days when we need to make a price reduction because the home hasn't sold at that higher amount."

6. **It proves and demonstrates that you are a professional.** The bottom line is you're either a true pro or you're not. If you can't figure out what somebody will make on a deal, you're not a true pro. Do the math. Talk about the numbers. This will eliminate a lot of headaches later in the relationship.

7. **Your listing agreements can be considered invalid and unenforceable without a signed copy of the net sheet.** I'm pretty sure your listing contract says you're going to provide a net sheet, so make sure you do.

8. **Our sellers' service pledge states we will provide our sellers with one.**

9. **It makes closings anti-climactic.** Have you ever been to a closing and not known how much your seller will get? Truthfully, have you ever been to a closing, and the other agent hasn't told the seller how much they're going to get? I've been there. It's anti-

climactic. The last thing you want is for a seller to be confused or upset because they thought they were getting more at closing. When we go to a closing, it's nothing more than picking up a check for the expected amount. If you don't know how to fill out a net sheet, work on it.

10. **It protects you from inaccurate payoffs and estimates.** If a seller believes he will net 20 grand, but you don't have them sign the net sheet, and your seller only nets 15 grand because his payoff is $5,000 more, who are they pissed at? You. Have them sign the net sheet because you're done if they get a different payoff than expected. They're going to be angry, and they're going to blame you. The net sheet is a great protection, risk-reduction device.

11. **It helps you introduce inspection issues and needed repairs.** I always put 1,000 bucks in on my net sheet for inspections and repairs. I say, "Oh my gosh, your home is so fabulous, Mr. and Mrs. Seller, but homes in this area tend to bring $2,000 to 3,000 worth of inspection issues." Do it upfront. I hate selling a home twice. You sell it once to the buyer, and then you have to sell it again at the inspection. Put a dollar amount in the net sheet for inspections and repairs.

12. **It helps you negotiate a higher fee.** Thus, increasing your profitability. A net sheet will help you negotiate a higher fee because there's certainty in the numbers. They get it. They see that if you split equally, you're paying a buyer's agent as much as you're paying yourself. Why would I pay myself less than a buyer's agent? That doesn't make any sense. Do you want the

person representing your interest to be paid less than the person that's negotiating against you?

13. **It helps your sellers get comfortable with negative equity.** Guess what? Sellers are bringing money to closing. "Are you kidding me? I need to bring 6,000 to closing?" "Yeah, it's okay." Use this line to close on a seller thing, "You know what's funny, Mr. and Mrs. Seller? When your IRA account went down 20,000 bucks, you didn't say one word." People will lose money in the stock markets and in retirement plans all day, but God forbid they lose a dollar on their home. Everybody has lost money in the stock market at one time or another if you're in it.

Using this analogy helps them rationalize having to deal with negative equity situations. Negative equity is no big deal. I do care, but I really don't care if you're bringing a check to closing because there are recurring expenses a seller will face in real estate. If you don't write a check now, you may be writing checks to hold the property for another year.

14. **It helps you explain prorated taxes.** If you don't already know how to figure them, learn how to figure them because they're a problem at closing.

15. **It helps you quantify seller concessions.** The time to talk about seller concessions is at the listing, upfront. Have you ever had sellers say, "I'm not paying any closing costs. Not going to happen"? You don't want them to say that at the time you have an offer to kill the sale.

16. **It helps you get counteroffers written.** Use

the net sheet to do the math when sellers don't like an offer. "I don't know. It isn't enough."
"Well, good, let's figure it, and then let's figure out your new number when we do the counter."
"Oh, well, that number looks good."
"Great. Sign here, thank you." That's the counter; it's done.

17. **It helps you convince the seller not to hold onto their home.** Again, let's assume a negative equity situation. "What's the home costing you a month to hold onto?" Let's say it's three grand, and the net's six grand. You hold onto it two more months; guess what, you're at zero. You must get sellers to acknowledge the cost to hang onto property, especially with vacant homes.

I did $900,000 on a sale, and we covered taxes, insurance, and maintenance. There was no mortgage on it, but it's still a few thousand bucks to maintain a home like that. They're complaining about six grand. I'm like, "Do you know how many months it takes to sell a $900,000 property? It could easily cost you 24 grand if you hold onto it."

18. **It should be done with every counter.** Every counter should have a net sheet. A seller cannot make an informed and educated decision without considering the real numbers. Certainty is established by doing this. We all know sellers want certainty!

19. **It helps you restructure a transaction.**
Maybe we don't do 3 grand in cost, but two grand. We'll just restructure this transaction. Sometimes you

can get a lower sales price that nets the seller more money.

Some sellers are so egotistical; they're like, "I want to have the higher price, but I'll pay more in fees because I've got to have the higher price." It's weird, but it helps you restructure, and it shows that you know your business and creates certainty. Understand that principle balances do not include monthly interest.

20. **On a short sale, banks require them.** Short sales are cyclical. It is when a bank takes a payoff that is short of what the balance is. They will not accept a short payoff unless you have a clean, well-documented, well-demonstrated net proceeds sheet.

21. **It shows you know your business and creates certainty!**

Now do ten net sheets for people and have your broker or title company review them for accuracy. You should be able to pull out a napkin and do the net proceeds if you are a real Source of Sales Pro.

12

SELLER OBJECTIONS

Let's talk about the number one biggest problem real estate agents have: handling objections. So many people have trouble handling commission objections. However, there are also small objections that people come up with when listing a property.

What is your belief about objections? If you're getting objections, that means you're in business. That means you're doing real estate. Anybody who is in real estate and doesn't have an objection is not in business. They're not seeing clients.

About Objections

- **Most of them can be handled within a minute if handled properly.** Think about the highest paid, most skilled salespeople and how much they make each minute they handle and master every objection. $5000 in commission in 1 minute easy. I've seen agents throw away more in less time.
- **If you're getting objections, that's good.**

Objections mean the client is engaged and seriously considering doing business with you! That is GOOD! Your goal each day is to handle ten or more objections from prospects. You do that, and you'll be rich!

- **Think about how much you can lose by not being a good objection handler.** When people object to you, and you're terrible at converting objections, how much money does it cost you? $5,632, which is an average commission. If I'm not good at handling objections, it could cost me five grand every time. Now, let me ask you, how much money do you make for every no that you hear? 94 bucks. No's are good, but handling objections is better.
- **Figure out, in time, your per hour cost or income**. I know that if I was educated, practiced, rehearsed, and anticipated objections from a buyer or seller, I could be highly paid. If I handle an objection in a minute, I could make $5,600 in one minute. People lose thousands of dollars because they don't know how to handle objections. First, don't freak out; it means they want to do business with you. If you're not being objected to, you're not in business. Sales is a high-contact sport. Go out and make your contacts and get your objections.
- **It stops momentum and creates bad emotions if handled poorly.** The bottom line is that if you don't handle objections properly, it can create some bad emotions and cost you a sale.

SOURCE OF SALES (SOS)

6-Step Process to Handling Objections

The Objection-Handling System was given to me by one of my mentors, Tom Hopkins, the author of *How to Master the Art of Selling*. If you use the following Objection-Handling System, you will be able to handle any objection by any buyer or any seller.

1. Hear them out.
2. Feed the objection back

- To feed a concern back to potential clients, all you need to do is repeat it back to them with a sincere questioning tone in your voice.

3. Question the concern.

- Ask them to elaborate on or clarify their concern. Do it seriously.

4. Answer the objection

- I feel very confident in telling you that throughout your career, everything you sell will have a few features or weaknesses you wish it didn't have,
- Champions study the weak points their offering has, and they learn how to handle the situation.

5. Confirm the answer

- After you've answered the objection in a way you feel should overcome it, confirm that you have
- "That clarifies this point, don't you agree?"
- "That's the answer you're looking for, isn't it?"

6. Change gears, and immediately go to the next step in your selling sequence or on to the next objection or concern they raise.[1]

The Truth About Objections

Some objections CAN'T be overcome.

- If I don't like or trust you.
- If they are not on the same page.
- If they can't afford to do **business.**
- If the answer is not in their best interest.

All objections CAN be overcome

- If they do like and trust you.
- If you are all on the same plan.
- If they in fact can do it.
- If the answer is in their best interest.

Tips for Answering Objections

Be clear and <u>concise</u>: People don't want BS; people want answers. I recently had an agent come up and say, "Hey, I'm getting ready to have a meeting with the seller. I told her to list it at $525,000. I told her to put in granite. I told her to strip the wallpaper. Well, she did the granite and the wallpaper, but I reduced it 50 grand! What am I going to tell her?"

What does that seller want from you? They want an answer. What do you tell that seller? This is the key to being a great listing agent. If you're going to be a big-time lister, here's what you need to be able to say - *I was wrong*.

Is the seller going to respect you more if you sit there and puke all over them with statistics and blah, blah, blah, blah, blah? Or if you say, "Hey, you know what? I was wrong. I misread the market; I was wrong." Do you think I've told a seller that before? I certainly have. After the seller knew I had the guts to say, "I was wrong, I missed it," they trusted me. The agent who is never wrong often creates mistrust, apprehension, and a lack of influence with their client.

Speak with confidence: Most of the listings I get are second and third time around listings because I'm clear, I'm concise, and I deliver certainty. When I walk into a listing, people go, "Glenn is going to tell you the way it is." You know what, we've all missed the mark.

Look at them in the eye: You've got to look the seller in the eye and be clear and concise and say, "I was wrong. I missed it." The seller is more apt to keep you as their listing agent if you look them in the eye and say, "I was wrong." If you sit there and go, "Well, you know the five other comps we did, the part, the square foot..." They're going, "Just give me an answer. You're an idiot. I'm not listening to you."

Here's the way you soften it. "Mr. and Mrs. Seller, here's the thing, I care about you and like you so much that sometimes I become over-anxious. I become a little more optimistic because I like you so much; I wanted to get you maybe more than it was worth."

Have you ever listed a property for somebody that you really loved? You overprice it by 50 grand because you love them so much. It used to happen to me all the time; I love my people. I try not to do it anymore. I try to hit them upfront with what the market will really bear.

The point is, always say, "Well, Mr. and Mrs. Seller, you said the price was important, I was trying to get you the highest possible price I could get you, and I was wrong. I was overzealous. I overdid it. I shouldn't have done it. I was wrong because I was just trying to get you the highest price. So now, Mr. and Mrs. Seller, we're going to have a meeting where we can go through it in detail, but this is your number." Here's the point, does it really take you more than 90 days to know what the number is on a home? No.

When I get a listing that the price reduction meeting happens in 60 or 90 days, I tell my sellers upfront, "We can try at this higher amount, but I'm going to tell you what your home is going to sell for in 30 days. Will you be better off if we sell your home in 30 days, or do you want me to sit here and lie to you and tell you what your number isn't? Let's set that expectation. Can we have a real honest conversation? Can I be clear and concise about where you need to be in 30 days?"

Would your listings be better if you talked to sellers like that? Would they appreciate it if you did that? Yes, they would. Speak with conviction. Don't waffle. You might be wrong again. Trust me, I've done that. Look them in the eye. You have conviction, and you're clear and concise. People want answers. That's what people value, and that's what they want from you.

Don't make them wrong. When handling objections, don't make your seller wrong, EVER! The real skill, and the SOS approach, is to be able to help a seller recognize and admit that their perspective was incorrect. Use the word "incorrect" in business and in life. People's perspectives and decisions can be formed much easier in this context than in the context of right and wrong.

Answer with a question. The ol' porcupine technique; put it back on your seller to answer themselves. Sometimes you will be amazed at what a seller decides to do, especially in your favor! "Your commission is too high (seller)," "my commission is too high (the agent)?"

I will teach you more about 21 ways to beat the commission objection later in the book. If that is all you say and engage them with your eyes and smile, the commission objection can be handled within seconds!

Tell them they are making a good <u>decision</u>.

SOURCE OF SALES (SOS)

Certainty in the transaction, as I say time and time again in this book, is what sellers and buyers want most. If you feel they are making a good or great decision, TELL THEM! Your clients want you to exude confidence and certainty.

Being a master of the seller will make you an enormous amount of money, it will save you time, and it will double your opportunity to get two-sided transactions. There's nothing better than doing both sides of the deal.

Seller Mastery: SOS Challenge

To begin Seller Mastery, complete the exercises in the *SOS Playbook*. If you don't already have your *SOS Playbook*, visit www.glennbill.com/sosplaybook to download your copy.

To begin applying your Seller Mastery to your business, complete the exercises in the *SOS Playbook*. Within this section, you will find a Saleability checklist that you can use with sellers, along with journal questions for you to respond to.

PART IV

BUYER MASTERY

It is one of the oldest questions in real estate: Do you prefer to work with buyers or sellers?

It always amazes me how many people say they prefer to work with buyers. I am not here to talk you out of working and mastering buyers at all, but you need to be more skilled than ever to make representing buyers a profitable venture. Buyer representation in the hottest of markets can be brutal. Late nights, weekends, lines to show outside of listings, and multiple offers threaten your ability to be profitable. When on the losing end, hot markets threaten your ability to maintain a positive relationship and keep your buyer loyal to you.

Although an argument can be made that you need to be a more skilled agent to be a listing agent, I have found that once you have a system for listing, the ability to duplicate and scale listing success is quite easy.

Scaling buyer success is quite a different challenge. To be a killer buyers' agent takes much more skill, versatility, hard work, and market knowledge, not to mention peak negotiation skills and influential closing ability.

As a buyers' agent, you don't win every deal like you do when you are the listing agent. Therefore, what I teach you in the coming chapters will make you a much better buyers' agent, a more well-versed agent, and an agent who will rarely lose in multiple offer situations.

When you list, you only need to know about the one property you are listing. Buyers' agents need to be able to assess value, neighborhoods, amenities, and potential pitfalls on the fly every day from neighborhood to neighborhood.

Learning how to be a master of buyers is not easy. It is hard work, but once you master it, you will be an invaluable (and highly paid) asset to your future clients!

13

SETTING THE TABLE WITH BUYERS

Don't Get Worked Over

- Have you ever had a buyer work you to death then purchase a home without you, or worse, with another agent? How about the buyer that wants to lowball every offer and refuses to be reasonable in terms of value and the aspects of negotiation?
- Ever had a buyer say they want a specific type of home only to fall in love with something totally different?
- Ever had a buyer say they were pre-approved but had never been to a mortgage lender?
- Have you ever had a buyer who was going to inherit a large cash sum or receive a large settlement for the price of the home or down payment?
- Why is it we believe people when they say they're cash buyers?

A few years ago, Forest Lucas's Hilbert Mansion was for sale. A janitor at a Catholic school was referred to me. Catholic schools don't pay anybody anything, but he had a big sum, an inheritance, a big payout. I Googled him, and sure enough, where he said he worked was where he worked. I took him out to a nice lunch, I spent like $100 on it, and he was in his janitor outfit.

We go out and do plans, and I get my builder. We fawn all over this guy. His family has walked into the home going wow.

I start to think I'm getting worked by somebody who doesn't have money. So, I hire a private investigator to check it out. The guy was living in a Motel 6 on Pendleton Pike. There's no way he was qualified to own this property. This guy's a janitor at a Catholic grade school. I am a real estate sales god, or at least I think I am. Twenty-two years in the business, and I fall to this guy, right? I'm pretty good at spotting real vs fake when it comes to buyers, so if it can happen to me, it can happen to you.

Here's the great thing about real estate. This business will set you up to be rejected and fail in the most interesting ways. At the end of it, it's a great story. So, even though I spent a bunch of money, the laughs I get from that story are worth it.

Have you ever had a buyer who gets cold feet and wants out of the purchase? Have you ever had a buyer say, "If it's meant to be, it'll happen?" When they say that, respond with, "You know what, I totally agree with you. If it's meant to be, it's meant to be. So, here's what I think we should do. Let's offer the full price for the home and see if it's meant to be."

Have you ever had a buyer who expects you to show homes all the time on their time, and if you're not there, they threaten to leave you for an agent who will be there all the time? Don't like them? It's okay, fire them. Bye-bye. That's handled in an upfront conversation.

I will show my buyer so many homes, they'll be so tired

SOURCE OF SALES (SOS)

and exhausted they're going to ask me to pick the house. That works well. How many people have that philosophy? It's not sustainable, and I said to myself, I don't think I want to do business that way.

If you don't have a pipeline, you need to show as many homes as possible because you're building product knowledge. One of the seven fundamentals of sales and real estate is product knowledge. So, if you have some slouch buyer with you, who cares? At least you're going out and showing property and wearing them down. Once you've got four deals in your pipeline, that's going to end. I will give you the language that you can tell people, even if you don't have four deals. You might not be interested in showing 25 homes. I'm going to give you some language today that's going to help you dump a buyer and/or make them decide to buy in ten showings or less.

The bottom line is not to let buyers dominate your time. They will run you out of the business. You have a family to spend time with, and you have to have some me-time. Do you control the customer, or do they control you? I want you to have a renewed passion in controlling your business instead of your business controlling you.

Have you ever had a buyer call you on your listing and purchase it on the spot? I have. I needed to pay for my daughter's wedding. You know it's about 30 grand. I was going, "$30,000! I don't have $30,000." I had listed this great home for $319,000 on Sunday at 9 am. Did I want to take this call? Of course not, but I did. The person on the other end appreciated so much that I answered and would get them in ASAP that they went ahead, wrote an offer, and closed the sale. That fee totaled about $18,000 and got me that much closer to walking my daughter down the aisle! Question: How much money have you let go unanswered?

By the way, the most profitable calls you get will be Sunday morning because the wealthiest people in the world are working during the week. They're not getting an inheritance, so they don't have time during the week. The only time they have to shop for homes is Saturday and Sunday.

Leads that come in on Saturday and Sunday are usually from people who have jobs and income, which is a great thing to work with. Sunday morning calls = money. You get calls on a Sunday morning, I know you might have church, but there's a lot of money to be made there. So, what do I do? I answer the phone, I go out and show the home. Certainly, I am not suggesting or telling anyone not to honor their religion. I am just saying if there is a night service or a different time of service, you may want to be willing to adjust.

Have you ever had a buyer come into your open house and go, "I love it! I'm going to go get my husband." Bringing him back, "Well, I don't know. I mean if you love it, I guess we can buy it." "Great! You stay away, I'll deal with her." I love it when that can happen with buyers. Buyers are good. Buyers are good, and buyers' agents are great because I view being a buyer's agent like a Christmas present. If I know the market, it is kind of really freaking cool to walk somebody in the home that they're going to spend the next five to ten years in. They're always going to think of you and say, "I thank God for you. You're the agent that found my home."

Do you know what's really sad? When I list the home after some other agent has sold them the home and never followed up because they don't understand branding or client marketing services. I always say, "Who sold you the home?" and they go, "Gosh, I can't remember, I don't know, an agent from ABC Realty...uh, what was her name? Marge or something?" Don't be that agent. Understand that when you represent a buyer, how special and emotional it is and how much of a hero you are when you get the home. Make sure that when somebody buys a house through you, you give them a special gift, something meaningful. Any person you have found and sold a home to should never leave you. It's their home. Do you know how awesome and special that is to be able to do that? Should they decide to sell, they think of you to help them.

Have you ever had a buyer that bought in ten showings or less? Love them extra hard.

I want you to realize it's okay to show 20 or 30 homes. If you don't have four transactions in your pipeline, show 20 or 30 homes. It's about creating an expectation with the buyer that I'm the expert, I know the market, I'm going to show you the ten best homes in the market, and I have a feeling maybe one of these could be for you.

The Set-Up

These are questions you should be asking buyers when you first meet them. You want to ask these questions to know if you are showing and working with the right type of buyer! The last thing you want to do is work with the wrong buyers because they will suck the life out of you and run you out of enthusiasm for this business fast. Work with these questions if you want to set yourself up for buyer success. They will help you close buyers fast.

1. *Have you ever purchased a home before?* That is an important question because you really become the expert if they haven't. If they have, you need to understand what went on before they did it the last time. You need to ask them, "How was that experience? What did you learn? How would you like to see it go?" The reason you ask them those questions is a lot of times they'll say, "We looked at like 40 freaking homes, and I don't have the time; I'd like to look at ten homes and write an offer." Perfect, now we're on the same page. So, you need to ask that question.

2. *Are you aware of how we work **together**?* Buyers don't always know how we work together. Buyers think you put a key in a hole, open a door, and go, "Do you want to buy it?" That's not how we work together. That's how you serve them. That's how they dictate to you what you're doing. The question is, how good are you at communicating? If a buyer meets you, "So, what do you do for me? Why should I use you?" Can you rattle off 21 things you do for a buyer? Well, hopefully, by the end of this section of SOS, you're going to be able to.
3. *At the end of our discussion, I'm going to ask that you hire me as your **REALTOR**. Will that make you uncomfortable?* That's a closing question. A lot of us aren't closing buyers. Here's our buyer relationship. "Hi, I'm calling about 123 Main Street. Yes, $250,000, would you like to see it?" Great. Boom, done. That's your relationship.

None of these questions have even been asked. People call me on my listings, and I will run out there right now, and show the home. Especially if I don't have four deals in my pipeline, so I get it, it happens, but you know when I meet them, these questions come out.

Five Great Questions for Buyers

1. *If I find you the right home tomorrow, are you ready to purchase? What about within 30 days?* This lets you know if you are dealing with a buyer who has a time frame, who is motivated, and who, most importantly, won't waste your time looking.
2. *Are you willing to pay full price for a home if you love it?* Some buyers will refuse to pay full price, even in a

tough market. If they are not willing to pay full price, you are with the wrong buyer. This also sets the table for a full price or above full price offer when you are in the field. The time to talk about full price offers is not when you are standing in the living room of a home with ten people waiting to get in and two offers already on the home. Your buyers need to be set in a mind-frame that if it's the right home, they will step up and own it!

3. *Is there anyone else other than you or me who would prevent you from moving forward on a property that is right for you?* Third-party experts can be the death of us. You need to know if your buyers will be using a third-party expert to decide so that can get dealt with now! Usually, these third-party experts are the mom, dad, uncle, cousin, best friend, or group of friends. You are the expert, not them. You need to vet this out and eliminate it ASAP for a smooth relationship and successful buyer purchase.

4. *In a perfect world, how and when would you like to see this process end?* People need to communicate with you what the end game is. Starting with the end in mind is a great strategy for most business decisions! You will get two different answers to this question. If they are unclear, your process and your experience with them will be unclear and perhaps take forever. If they are clear with a specific deadline and date to close, you know you have some excellent prospects in front of you.

5. As a team, we will make this happen together. *What is the most important thing that I should know as your teammate?* See, what you know and how much more you know than your prospect doesn't really matter. Unless you uncover the most important things to your prospect, they will never listen to all

the fantastic things you have to say. On a rare occasion, however, these prospects will give you something of value and may help you learn or create a new way of doing something that serves their purpose!

The above questions will set you up for success, but never forget that the most important thing to a buyer is getting the **lowest price**!

14

21 WAYS TO PROVIDE SERVICE

You're going to know all these, but how well do you know them, and are you able to rattle them off? This really gets to the core of why someone should use you as a real estate agent. This chapter shares some great ways to explain why a buyer should use you as an agent.

21 Ways I Service You, The Client

1. I help you to negotiate the **best** price. Anyone can say that, but do you have a specific bullet point ready to show how you negotiate the best price? Here are a few of mine:

- I make great friends with the other agent.
- I know the comps and adjustments better than anyone.
- I create options and alternatives for financing so the price can be more affordable.
- I give offers that close quickly and are certain. No ambiguous terms.

- I understand what the seller really wants and give it to them.

2. I educate you on the current active **marketplace**. "We've seen everything on the market, would you agree that this is the best home? Great, then let's go ahead and buy it." Some people don't want to buy homes because they think maybe there's a deal down the road, perhaps they've missed something, so you want to constantly say we've seen everything on the market. "We're up to date. I've put everything in front of you that meets the needs you expressed to me. How about we pick the best one. Is this the best one? Great, let's move ahead."

3. I help you select a **property**. "If you're interested in saving time, let me do the work. I can make sure the homes don't back up to shopping centers or train tracks. There are problems with those properties. Let me show you the best properties."

It's easier to sell homes when you get the buyer in the mindset where they trust their agent and realize you're saving them time and bringing them the best properties in the market. Then you always tell them when you have the ten, "I've been through the market, I got the ten best properties, and I've got a feeling that yours is in here. I'm going to put a little star on the back of one of them, and when we're done looking today, if you pick the one that has the star on it, you're going to be a winner." So, what is their expectation?

Their expectation is that there is a winner in there. People would go out and be like, "Is this the one?!" The wife would be like, "Did you put the star on this one?" I didn't put the star on any of them, okay, until it was the one they loved. Then I would turn and put a star there on the back. "You picked the right one. Congratulations!"

It's called thinking outside the box. It's called selling. If they don't want it, they're not going to buy it. Somebody's not going to buy it just because I put a star on the back of it. When you go out to show homes, you go out to show homes. I don't go out to show homes. I go out to sell homes. "Glenn, I want to look at homes." Oh, I'm sorry, I don't look at homes. I sell homes.

Every buyer I've had this year calls me and says, "We want to buy this home." That's how I work with buyers. I don't show homes. If you want to look at homes and examine inventory, you go to my buyer's agent. Show the homes if you're new and don't have four deals in your pipeline. If you're experienced and a big producer and want to leverage and mass produce in real estate, only work with buyers if they know what they're buying or if you can say, "You need to buy this home." With my buyers, I call them and say, "I found your home," and they go, "Love it, when can we go?" I take them there and ask, "This is what you want, right?" "Yep." "Let's buy it."

4. I help you get a 24-hour **loan pre-approval**. We all know a lender that will get you 24-hour loan approval, especially if you're good. That's big. "Do you think there's an advantage to going in and getting the lowest price if you're pre-approved for a loan or even fully approved? Of course, there is."

5. I provide you with **comparable** sales at the time of the offer. "I want to let you know before we write on this, here's the highest sale, here's the lowest sale, here's the average sales price. Right now, your property is the highest home in the subdivision. Are you okay with that? We may have an appraisal problem. Are you cool with that? Are you willing to pay above the appraisal? Let's talk about all that before we write the offer. Do you love the home?" Remember, it's an emotional buy; it's not a logical buy. If they're in love, they're in love. You're not going to trade in your spouse because she costs too much, right? You love her. All right, same thing.

6. I explain property taxes and how they're used to **decrease** the money you need to put down. "Do you have any idea how property taxes can be structured in an agreement to help you bring less to closing? Well, you can do that. We have what's called tax proration, and I can prorate plus help you create a situation where you need less money down. Does that sound like something you'd be interested in?"

7. I explain **earnest** money procedures. Earnest money can present a huge customer stall when trying to get a purchase agreement signed. It can also create a lot of ill will in the event the deal falls through, and you need to get it back. Make sure you are an expert at earnest money, how to explain it, how to use it, and how to make it a non-issue in the sale so you can proceed to close.

8. I write the purchase **agreement** on your new home. Anyone can write a purchase agreement, but how you write your agreements versus the rest of the

SOURCE OF SALES (SOS)

agents in your marketplace matters. Quick time frames, proper documentation, and proper questioning of the listing agent to get an offer written the way the seller wants to see it gives you the best opportunity to win the sale versus the other agents who may be interested.

9. I introduce you to a new home **builder**. If you're not working builders, you're crazy. Builder business is huge. Pick up a builder this year. It'll be a good idea for your business; you'll make money.

10. I assist with lot **selection**. What does every new home builder want to sell you? The worst lot. "Oh, this is a premium lot." It is? What do all new home salespeople tell you when you're interested in a lot? "We have three other people getting ready to put a reservation on this lot." They do this. Excellent sales technique, but you need somebody. So, you tell them that story. Then say, "And, that's why you need me, that's why I want to work with you."

11. I explain the process of **building**. Building a home is a very complicated and detailed process. It is a totally different experience than helping a buyer with a resale product. A buyer and you (the agent) need to understand that the builder reps you deal with represent the builder, not the buyer. They are very skilled and trained at leveraging the NEW HOME against your buyer's emotions.

Things like lot selection, lot premiums, upgrades, base included finishes are all very important decisions that need to be addressed when building. Perhaps one of the biggest issues with builders is their contracts, and the ability to manipulate time frames, products, and house locations can crush a buyer's expectation and happiness. As an agent, becoming prolific in the new home building process is an absolute must to represent clients, create rapport with the sales reps for even more sales, and get those buyers closed on a new home.

12. I will show you the properties. Now, I'm not going to show you properties, but somebody on my team's going to show them to you. If I don't have four deals in my pipeline, I'll show them to you.

13. I enlist you in **real-time** searches. Everybody knows how to do a real-time search for a buyer. The agent searches through the local board MLS systems where, if the buyer wants a four-bed, 2 1/2 bath in northern Washington township, it automatically emails them real-time searches when properties hit the market. Everybody can do that, but nobody tells them about it, so you should.

14. I help you determine the best **loan** programs. Here's the deal: Buyers don't know anything about financing. I stay out of financing and let my loan people do their business, but there are instances where a buyer needs a little guidance from me. If you really want to become an expert, you want to become an advocate for your buyer. If you want to be seen as somebody who cares, start referring people to 15-year loans and then see what they do ten years from the day you referred them on that 15-year loan. They'll tell you how much they love you and how much they'll never leave you.

Ten years ago, I started selling 15-year loans hard to

my buyers, and the thank you notes, the emails, the "Glenn, I can't believe you cared so much," started rolling in. It's one of the best forced savings programs you can ever be a part of. Talk to people about a 15-year loan; no other REALTORs talk about it. It's going to set you apart, and it's going to differentiate you. At a minimum, if they say no, they're going to go, "Our REALTOR really cares about our financial well-being."

15. I recommend **inspectors.** Having the right inspector who is reputable and known in the market works to your advantage. Introducing a novice with no branded awareness creates uncertainty and can cost you a deal. Make sure you look for an inspection company that has a strong warranty tied to it for risk reduction.

16. I negotiate inspections. "I'm going to talk to you about the inspection process for buying a new home and used home."

17. I provide good faith estimates/cost estimate worksheets. We all know certainty is the name of the game when buyers and sellers are making decisions. You MUST deliver real numbers that are correct and verified so your client and the other parties all have confidence that the deal will close. This is a sign of a real pro! Know your numbers.

18. I provide you with home **warranty** information. As stated above, warranties are excellent risk-reduction tools. To know how to present them and get them in your transaction only makes things stronger and your life easier after the sale. Get very familiar with two or

three of these companies; they can also be a referral partner for you!

19. I educate you on short sales and **foreclosures**. Now, when people call and say, "I'm interested in buying short sales and foreclosures." What do you say? "No." Let me refer you to another agent who can work with you on short sales and foreclosures. I'm sure you can find a handful of agents in your marketplace. They usually say, "I specialize in short sales." I do short sales, but I do them my way, and they work by my rules. I set the expectations up clearly.

20. I save you time and only **show** you what you want to see. You're going to get a whole bunch of problems and end up spending more than you want and be upside down on your property. Let's buy a home that's ready to move into that you don't even have to worry about so you can live your life.

If they want to see foreclosures, I find the worst three I can show them, and I'm like, "Here's this beauty. You're going to have fun for the next three years fixing this up when you guys could be going to Florida, enjoying each other, enjoying life. You're going to be married to your home. Oh, you know what, I have one home I might want to show you that's in perfect condition and priced really well." You walk them in, and they go, "We love it!" I'm like, "Hey, let's not do all that work," Boom, done. So, if they want to do that, take them to three bad ones, then show them the best property, and you'll sell them. That's only four showings or less.

You want to get to the point where you're not *an*

expert; you're *the* expert. You want your buyer to go, "Man, this guy knows the inventory." The problem is we have real estate agents in our business and in our culture that act like they're experts, but they're not. They don't know the inventory. So, when you go, " I'm showing 40 homes, and they're not buying." I would say it's because you don't know the inventory. You should be out looking at the 40 homes without them.

Let me give you a fascinating tidbit. Have you ever shown a buyer several homes, and nothing's right? I've got a great solution to that problem. Up their price by $50,000, and they'll love everything. "I know that you hate everything that I show you, so I'm sure you're very fascinated with this problem, right? Let me show you some stuff that's $50,000 more. It's going to be another couple hundred bucks a month." We'll talk about the money and overcome their objections after they fall in love with a home because it's an emotional sale. So, move them up in price if they give you permission. Do it, and then boom, they find the right home.

21. I preview properties. This is the number one most important thing you can do. As a new agent, if you don't have a pipeline, get out there and look at homes. Be prepared. We sell homes, so know your product. What I hate the most is when I have this conversation with a new agent:
"How long have you been in business?"
"Three months."
"How many homes have you previewed?"
"Well, none. I went to a broker's open house, I ate lunch there, but I didn't really look at the home."
Okay, if you don't know what to do in real estate, is it

easy to preview homes? Stop choosing the choice of it's easy not to. Get out and preview homes in the specific marketplace you want to dominate. Go out and preview the listings that are in your company.

If you have no product knowledge, you will fail as a salesperson. You will not be an expert. You will not be able to speak intelligently. You will not attract people who go, "I have to do business with that guy." You want to be able to say, "I was in 15 homes this week, and out of the 15, these three were the best for what you want." When you start previewing homes, people will come into your life that will buy them. I've done this with agents for 20 years. You look at waterfront homes, what happens? You have that product information. You have that information on the inventory. You're much more apt to recognize an opportunity for somebody who wants to buy on the water.

If you don't know the inventory, you can't sell it. If you don't know the inventory, you aren't going to sell many homes. So, get out there and preview homes.

15

INFLUENCING YOUR BUYERS

You must put yourself in front of **buyers** and give **value** first.

Are there areas around you that you haven't branded? Let's say it's The Bristols. Check to see if "The Bristols" is branded by any agents yet on Facebook. If not, start a page, start posting, and capture the interest of everyone who lives there or wants to move there. Demonstrate your expertise on The Bristols.

I don't know what neighborhood you live in or what neighborhood you work in, but I suggest putting a Facebook page up. Give value first. Help people to realize that if they are looking to get in this neighborhood, you are the value provider because you know what's going on there. If you'd like to sign up for my real-time search on anything that happens in this neighborhood, give me your email address, and I will forward you information right now. If you live in this neighborhood and you want to know what homes are active in this neighborhood, I'll put you on a real-time search and send you every single active listing that comes up."

Let me give you this as a contact management thing. I ask clients we've sold houses to if they would like real-time searches about what happens in their neighborhood. If they live in Shady Manor, I put them in as a buyer prospect, and anything in Shady Manor, once I sell them that home, they're getting automatic emails from me that I don't even touch. I'm providing value, they're seeing what's going on in their neighborhood, and they're thinking, "Glenn is the expert." If they even get a tiny inkling about selling their home, they look at what I'm saying about Shady Manor first.

Providing Value to Buyers

How do you get in front of buyers and provide value? Consider where you would go to find information about buying a home.

The first question I would ask is who are people talking to when it comes to making a change? Answer: their friends, other agents, lawyers, accountants, parents, loan originators, and hopefully, you!

The second question is, where are they going to find information about moving? Undoubtedly social media, Google, Zillow, and any number of periodicals and websites. Here is the point: Are you there? If not, put on your marketing cap and start becoming a contributor.

1. Run ads. Social Media advertising is the cheapest form of advertising there is. Start a campaign that is compelling and clickable, such as "Get my list of undervalued properties here." Trust me, people will call you.
2. Hyper-local websites. Do you own your favorite neighborhood's website or domain name? If not, you should. We own hundreds of neighborhood domain names and lease them to HOA's. Nothing is more powerful than starting a neighborhood

SOURCE OF SALES (SOS)

Facebook page or website and being able to cooperate with all the neighbors and HOA's.
3. Service-oriented websites. Create a first-time homebuyer website. What do people buying a home need? They need mortgages, agents to show them, contractor estimates, and insurance. Do you have a real estate sales blog that is a resource? If not, get one.
4. How about a first-time homebuyer seminar? Those are tough to pull off, but mortgage lenders are nice people. There are mortgage companies that will love to do first-time homebuyer seminars with you. Go to your local bank manager and get referrals from them.
5. Property Managers. No one has access to more first-time homebuyers than the property managers in your area. Have pizza nights, home buyers' seminars, or a property manager Facebook group to help them with their challenges. Property managers are gold, but you must deliver value to them first.
6. Open Houses. Chapter 7 is all about this. Simply put, if you are not doing 48 to 52 homes a year, then you should be participating in open houses a minimum of two out of four weekends per month.

Finding the Motivated Buyer

1. They **must** have financing.
2. They **must** have a time frame.
3. You **must** set the stage.

- Qualification question: "If you find the right home, are you willing to write an offer in the next 30 days?"
- Preview homes and pick the best.
- Tell them, "I think I found your home."

Questions that Identify and Increase Buyer Urgency

Understanding, creating, and determining buyer urgency will help you distinguish the lookers from the doers! You need to determine if the people in front of you are willing to do business. Do not do business with unmotivated buyers, period. The following will help you determine if the buyers you are working with are time wasters or moneymakers.

This is a skill the best of the best use, and it makes them more productive and profitable than all their competition. Think about it, how long does it take you to cut a potential buyer loose? How much time have you wasted on buyers? Top producers do it in one meeting!

1. *If I find you a home in the next 30 days, are you willing to write an offer?* I've mentioned this question multiple times. Let's start asking that question more. If you don't have four transactions in your pipeline, you don't necessarily need to ask it, but you should ask it. If they say no, that's fine. Here's the deal, even if somebody doesn't have a timeline and they fall in love, they're going to buy the home. So, if you don't have four deals in your pipeline, roll the dice and go show them properties because you should be previewing properties every day because it improves your product knowledge.
2. *Will we meet in my* **office** *or at your* **home** *before we start the process?* I know it is easy to meet with people at the office. Is it easier not to meet with them and

SOURCE OF SALES (SOS)

just go ahead and start showing them homes while not asking them engaging questions and letting them run you all over the city? It's not easier. It's easier if you meet them first and ask them engaging questions. We all think it's easier to just start the relationship and start showing homes, and maybe they'll just buy that home right now in ten showings or less. It happens occasionally, but not as often as when you create a plan for how you'll work together.

3. *Can you get **approved** before we start looking at homes?* "I'm already approved." What do you say when they're already approved? With whom? Can I get a phone number? Do you have an approval letter or email?

4. *Will you write an **offer** before we list and/or sell your home?* How many people don't have the guts to go ahead and let somebody buy a home because you're on the line to list their home? Gutless salespeople. "Let's go ahead and put our necks on the line together and buy this home. I will get your home sold." Man, that takes some guts. Let's stop being afraid; let's take some risks. It's not going to cost us anything except a bit of pride. You could put your client in financial ruin if you don't get it sold, but here's the key, if you're honest, you tell them to expect the worst case. Whenever I sell a home to a buyer, I say, "Don't buy this home unless you're willing to take X for your home." Aren't we all smart enough to know what 10% below market value is? I don't usually miss by 10%. If I do miss, at least I've made it for 10%. So, maybe you could start an ad that says, "Are you stuck in your home and want to buy before you sell? I specialize in helping people buy before they sell." Do you know

how many people say, "I didn't even know we could buy before we sell"? That's called giving value to the marketplace. A lot of times, lenders allow it. I'll have the seller escrow 3 to 4 months of payments for a buyer if the lender lets them. So, when I go to list the property, I say, "Here's the great thing, if we close on December 1st, your first payment isn't going to be due until February 1st. The seller will pay your February, March, April, and May payment. Surely, we can get your home sold by May. Do you guys get that?" That happens. Lenders don't necessarily like that. You must find somebody willing to do that or figure out a way to make it happen.

5. *How much do you want the property?* They may not know, but most of them will. Ask, "Are you willing to lose it over 1k, 5k, or 10k?" Ask them how they will feel without it.

6. *How will you feel if you get **outbid**?* The egomaniac client is not going to want to get outbid. Ours is an emotional sale. Get them talking about their feelings, and they may close themselves.

7. *How would you feel if you **lose this house**?* These questions deal with feelings and emotions. This is my favorite. Go for it and get the guts to ask them. Some people will say, "Do whatever it takes to get it." Those are the magic words you want to hear before going in to write the offer. Some agents don't ask that; they have NO idea how much the buyers want the home. When they don't get it for them, they lose a client!

8. *Are you willing to let **$1000** kill the opportunity?* How many buyers do you have that are willing to kill the opportunity to own a home over $1000? It happens. If somebody is willing to let a deal die

over $1000, you have a sales problem. We have an issue if we can't talk a buyer through a $1000 hurdle. That issue is probably going to be a trust issue. If you say this is the right decision, in the long run, you're going to make money, the $1000 isn't going to matter.
9. *What's your favorite **amenity** of this home?* People buy homes for the amenities, so focus on that. Do you really want to be without that?
10. *Do you really want to start over to re-find the **right** one?* Please say you don't want to start over. For many people, the time to start over and find a new home is not worth the $1000.

You are in control of your business. Provide value, establish yourself as the expert, and ask engaging questions that move your buyer in the right direction.

16

21 WAYS TO BUILD LOYALTY

I want you to become an expert at building loyalty. It goes beyond customer satisfaction. Think about it: Would you rather be satisfied by a job well done or loyal because the job was done exceptionally well and you want to experience that again?

What is customer satisfaction worth? Not much. Customer satisfaction is just above "you suck." Satisfied customers don't refer to you and don't go to bat for you. If they're just satisfied, it's not going to happen.

Loyal customers make sure that their family and friends do business with you. Loyal customers go, " John is the greatest real estate salesperson in the world. There's nobody better; you have to use John."

There are simple ways to build loyalty, but most agents won't do them. I believe you will because you want to have an exceptional real estate career.

Communicate...all the time. Are you willing to communicate every day with your clients? Are you willing to respond when they call you? Are you willing to answer a text at 10:00 pm? When my people call me, they get a response within 5 minutes, guaranteed. I've had clients text me late at night, and they can't believe I'm still responding. What do you think those people are telling their friends? They're going, "Glenn Bill works at 10:30 at night. If you want something, he gets it for you at 10:30." You might think that'll ruin your family life. It won't. If somebody's asleep, you just go to the bathroom and send a quick text back. Or ask your spouse to understand that if you are going to make a half-million dollars a year, you need to be able to communicate with your people when they need to hear from you so that you can build loyalty.

Establish a customer service model. What is your customer service model? Do you deliver the type of service you expect of others? When I'm a customer, I expect a high level of service because I give a high level of service. Poor, lousy service frustrated me, but I get fascinated by it now and think to myself, "Gosh, I'm so fascinated that you have no concept of what it means to serve your customer well."

Develop vendor loyalty. We all work with banks, inspectors, vendors, plumbers, and electricians. What are you doing to build loyalty with your vendors to maximize and capitalize on those relationships? There are programs you can do for your favorite vendors. Put them in place, and they'll be loyal to you.

Train yourself on loyalty. Have you read a book recently on customer loyalty? Jeffrey Gitomer has written a book called *Customer Satisfaction is Worthless, Customer Loyalty is Priceless*. It's a great book that really hits home on how to develop a loyal customer instead of just a satisfied customer.

SOURCE OF SALES (SOS)

Create customer incentives. I don't know if you have a customer incentive program. People are doing some unbelievable stuff. Go out, find 50 businesses, have them create discounts for your customers, create a card, send the card to all your customers, give them $500 worth of savings on whatever has to do with their home. That's an exceptional and pretty easy customer incentive program that costs you very little.

Increase customer's equity. "Here are some ideas, Mr. or Mrs. Seller, that will help raise the value of your home that will help limit unnecessary improvements."

Be reliable. Have you ever been referred and have messed up the referral, thus becoming too big of a risk to ever refer again? People are out there on your Facebook page, in your email list, and they're not directly saying they're referring people, but you blow over the lead because you just didn't get it. You're not reliable, you're going to be too much of a risk, and you're not going to be referred next time.

Value people over technology. Technology is great. However, when you bring in leads that are not ready to convert, it will not work. That's the problem with a lot of real estate agents. They know the technology, but don't know how to connect with people. Being personable is more important than being great with technology.

Be flexible. Customers are there to be served, not to serve you. There is nothing more annoying to a customer than to have a salesperson who displays no ability to be flexible. When it comes to schedules, offers, listings, time frames, and negotiation, remember selling is NOT telling; it is creating options and alternatives.

Know their names. The other day, I was in a listing, and the woman's name was Candace. I said, "Oh Courtney, I really appreciate the listing...Candace, Candace, I'm sorry." Make that mistake once, and you'll be forgiven. Make it repeatedly, and you won't have loyal clients. Have you taken Kevin Trudeau's Mega Memory Course? I have. It's helped me. What you do is create a picture for each new name you hear. For example, for Gary, I would think hairy. I'd see hair all over Gary's face, and I'd say Gary, Gary, Gary three times to myself. When I connect with Gary again, the hair image will help me remember his name. Put a picture on their face. For Bob, you might put a fishing pole on the guy's head with a bobber hanging down. Get the picture?

Get video testimonials. Get to know your clients well enough to know where they get their coffee or favorite lunch spot. Send a $25 gift card as thanks for a testimonial. Put those testimonials on your page, and when you go to list a home, say, "By the way, you might want to check my YouTube channel, so you don't have to hear me tell you about how great I am. Let me have some of my customers tell you how great I am." If I say it, they doubt it; if they say it, it's true. Make sure you're getting video testimonials.

Know and use your company's success story. You may be part of a very successful company. Leverage your company's success as a whole and other agents on your team.

SOURCE OF SALES (SOS)

Survey your clients. Do you send client surveys to your buyers and sellers? Don't you want to know what they're thinking? What are their needs? You can create surveys for free with Survey Monkey or even Google forms. Keep the number of questions short, five maximum, and use variety, like some multiple-choice questions, some yes/no, and some where they have to write something. Offer to send them the survey results so they can see what other clients of yours think, too. This is a great way to create engagement.

Contact them personally. It can be tempting to send a quick text or email but doing so all the time doesn't create loyalty. Sometimes, you create problems by not calling. Texting and emailing when there is a problem is not an appropriate way to make things happen unless it's a text to ask, "When is a good time for us to talk?"

Advise on brands, more than one. Several vendors put their fingers into our transaction. Your ability to know who is the best in the business of the many different vendors is a loyalty point that will carry over after the sale. If you refer a lousy vendor, that can lose you a client. If you refer a rockstar vendor, the client will be loyal for life.

Put on client gatherings. Your ability to help your clients increase their business outside of your transaction will create loyalty at the highest level. I have helped my clients and their kids find jobs, and I promote their non-profits. You do this, loyalty will follow.

Write up a Quality Service Pledge. We put our

service in writing. Do you put your service in writing? Do you give your client the right to fire you if you're not good? I always tell my people, "I'm not going to force you to work with me. If you don't want me to work for you, fire me, get rid of me."

Ask what your clients want upfront. As with any task, starting with the end in mind is a great idea, especially in the sale of real estate. Find out what they want and deliver on it!

Have empathy with your customers. Understand where they're coming from. People who want to do business will be loyal to you if you really understand and empathize with them and their situations. We all have bad stuff that goes on in our lives. We don't need to immerse ourselves in their junk, but we can be empathetic. Some clients are mean, rude, and abrasive. There's a reason they're mean, rude, and abrasive. If you can understand that and be empathetic towards them, that will help them be loyal to you. They'll say, "I was going through a real tough time, but my agent got it and created some great solutions for me and got me through it."

Send thank you notes. When was the last time you received a thank you note? How did it make you feel?

Offer rewards programs. An oldy but a goody. Do you have or could you create a rewards program for your new home buyer or seller where they receive discounts from ten different vendors, say carpet, windows, roofs, keys, supply stores, big-box retailers, local restaurants? You get the picture. Package ten local businesses in a program that offers discounts to your clients, and they will love you forever.

Those are 21 ways to create loyalty. Once you get started, you'll think of others. You can create loyalty however you want. Go to the *SOS Playbook* and answer the following questions. What's your loyalty program going to be? What are you doing to build loyalty with your buyers and sellers? Who are you loyal to and why? This is important because the same reason you're loyal is the same reason your customer is loyal. Think about your best-referring customer. What have you done for them that built their loyalty? Can you do it on a large-scale with all your clients?

17

CLOSING THE SALE

You cannot close the sale until you know the buyer's **wants and needs**. You learn what they want and need by properly qualifying and asking engaging questions. Real estate agents do not know how to ask questions in general. I can't wait for you to go out into the marketplace and make things happen with these questions.

What Motivates Them to Buy?

How do you know what they want? What motivates them to buy? You figure out the answers through proper qualification. It's what they want; it's not what **we** want that matters. You must radiate your **belief** and conviction that buying a particular home is a good decision for them.

Buying Signs

There are certain things buyers do and say when they're ready to go ahead with an offer. It's vital to your career success that you learn to recognize what buyers do to let us know they want to close.

- **Verbal** buying signs are positive comments or asking for technical information.
- **Visual buying signs include** lingering, relaxation, mentally moving in. Watch the actions of a couple. When they agree, you might see hugs, handholding, long stares, kisses, and loud comments. These are all good signs!
- **Pay attention to the Husband-Wife Analysis.** An example of these signs would be: They're walking through, they're lingering, they're sitting on the furniture, and they're going, "This is great, this is the one, I think this is it, I love this backyard. Do you know what the taxes are? Do you know what the utilities are?" Understand the buying signs and let them know it's time to close.
- **The best buying sign:** They want to see the home again. In my experience, eight out of ten times, if people want to see the house a second time, they're going to write an offer.

They Will Buy Commitment

I know they want it, so I will close this sale by...

- Asking confident questions. We want to help them rationalize. We want to deliver their needs with confidence. Buyers have a need for confidence. They need their agent to say, "I think it's a good buy. I think this is the one. This is the one I put a star on, I can't believe it. We're all in tune. We're in this together. We're a team. This is a blast."
- Helping them **rationalize** their decision.
- Delivering their need for **confidence.**
- We **pull** and **lead**, not **push** and **talk**. In my

illustrious sales career, I'll never forget when I really needed a fee, showing a good friend a home. We were down in the basement and there was this water heater that had this contraption on top of it. Never seen a water heater like that, and I said, "Man, that's a powerful water heater." I actually said that, and my buyer started laughing. That was being pushy. Not the way to sell; we need to pull and lead. When you're showing property, "Oh my God, it's such a good home, you really need to buy this, you're at an open house, oh my God, I think these other people want it."

- Ask questions, don't recite statements or facts. The more questions you ask, the better salesperson you are.

People like to do business with me because I am convincing, I'm believable, and we're in it together. They know they can trust me not to lead them to the wrong decision. After 25 years in real estate, my customers say, "Glenn, we'll do it if you say do it." That's awesome. So, if you're five or ten years in the business, imagine what your career could be like in ten years if you start delivering value and developing loyal clients. They start calling you and saying, "Hey, we found a home we want to buy." That's the type of business I want you to have.

Know How to Speak

Another thing I learned from Tom Hopkins was to pay attention to the effect our words have on people. Understand words, tones, sentence structure, and the need for a soft, nice voice. Doctors use words, attorneys use words, and salespeople use words. Some words kill your sale, like "Sign the contract."

Who wants to sign a contract? Not good words. Those create negative emotions. People don't want to sign, and they don't want contracts, but they will approve an agreement. They don't want to look at a down payment or a monthly payment. They want to look at the initial investment or the monthly investment. What you say can hurt. People do not want to buy, but they love to own. "Well, I'd really love you to buy this," versus, "I'd really love you to own this." In *Mastering the Art of Selling Real Estate*, Tom teaches about nasty words and good words.

Planned Pause

Once you ask for the **decision**, shut up! There are times when we have to shut up. Two things happen; they'll either **agree** with the decision or **object** to it. So, after you say, "Mr. or Mrs. Buyer, do you think this is the right home?" shut up. Don't say anything. They may go, "Yeah, I think it's right," or they may go, "I'm not sure." Then you will complete step one of the objection: Feed it back. Two, hear it out. Three, question the objection. Four, answer the objection. Five, confirm the answer. This is what professional salespeople know how to do. Six steps to handling objections. If they object to it, just handle the objection, and then shut up again.

Write the Offer

This is where new salespeople falter. "I know I did an offer in training, but I'm not sure I can do this offer. I do not want to write this offer in front of these people, I'm going to look so stupid." I have a tip for you. Write an offer every day until you're comfortable doing it with another new person. When I started in business, I had an investor that said, "Glenn, write five assumed no approval offers every day."

I wrote five offers a day for this investor. Why? I didn't have a pipeline, so I wasted my time. You know what? After writing twenty offers a week, I got pretty good with the form. If you're new, you should practice writing an offer every day. Write an offer on one of the big producer's homes, make up the name, hand it to the experienced agent, and say, "Hey, I got an offer on your property." They'll go, "What?!" Then say, "Oh, I was told to do this in SOS. Can you just review it and make sure that I did it right?" For those of you who are brand new, you need to be writing a minimum of one offer a day, fictitiously or not, until you're good, and then take it to your manager for review.

Once you know what you're doing, writing an offer takes about eight minutes. Write them and get them to your manager every day, and then the manager should go, "Yeah, it looks good." Now, you'll have gained confidence in writing them when the time is right. There's nothing worse than being terrified to pull out a purchase agreement when you're not sure how to write it.

What Is Closing the Sale?

> *"Closing is a well-filled pen in the hand of a sane and mature individual who affixes their signature on a predetermined dotted line with no physical help from the salesperson."*
> —J. Douglas Edwards

My definition of closing is the art of establishing rapport first and then, qualifying, presenting, handling areas of concern, and creating a symphony of words, good words, great words, beautiful words, and actions that emotionally build and culminate in a win-win situation and a final agreement. That's my definition of a closing. The closing for me really starts at the handshake. It's building that trust and doing all these different things.

Who loses when you don't close? The **seller** loses, your **family** loses, the **buyer** loses, and your **broker** loses, most importantly...you lose. We must move people from procrastination to commitment, and we do that with the purchase agreement. Start filling out that form by asking **reflex** questions.

A reflex question is a question that elicits an obvious answer, especially yes!

Reflex questions would be:

- Do you feel you would be better off with this home?
- Would your life be better if you had the equity in cash in your pocket?
- Would you like all the appliances?
- How would you feel if the seller paid all the closing costs?

Fill it out, then see how it looks. Then, get their signature!

Reflexive Techniques

As I show properties, I ask, "Do you want the refrigerator to stay?" They'd say, "yes." And I'd write it in. "Tell me what you're thinking about possession." "Seven days." I'd write it in. They would see me writing the purchase agreement.

Knowing the Numbers is a Must, Especially for the Prospect

If you're on a second or third showing, please have a cost estimate worksheet with you, too. If a buyer doesn't know what the monthly payment is and the minimum down payment is, they're probably not going to buy the home. Have it in writing from your lender on the second and third showing.

The more **earnest** money, the stronger the **sale**. I know we represent them and want to talk about less earnest money, but I'm all about big earnest money if you're in a competitive offer situation. My deals are easier, bigger, and smarter.

Closing Questions

Top salespeople who make over $125,000 average five major closes before they leave or buy.

The average salesperson knows two closes:

- Shall we go ahead?
- What do you think?

Closing questions are what move the sale forward. Here are a few examples:

- Do you think this home is right for you?
- Are you willing to buy this home tonight?
- Is there any information I can provide you today to help you make this decision sooner?
- Do you see yourself being happier in this home?
- Are there any more questions? (That's the greatest close.)

There are books on closing the sale. There are canned closes, but what you need to understand is there will be buyers that will have to sign a purchase agreement, and they're going to have to feel confident that it's a good decision for them. If you don't feel that way, they're not going to feel that way, and you're not going to sell the home.

Buyer Mastery: SOS Challenge

To begin mastering your buyers, complete the exercises in the *SOS Playbook*. If you don't already have your *SOS Playbook*, visit www.glennbill.com/sosplaybook to download your copy.

PART V

VALUE MASTERY

This is possibly the most fluid mastery session there is. Value is an ever-changing process, just as the market is. Certainly, there are value propositions that never change, and those are discussed in the pages ahead, but there are a few things you need to understand in today's world regarding value, how to deliver it, how to define it, and how to sell it!

1. REALTORS are being commoditized every day. There is a rush to figure out how to organize tasks, generate leads, execute marketing plans, and negotiate offers without you. This is happening daily. Your value will lay in your ability to be better, more personal, friendlier, and deeper than artificial intelligence.
2. You need to be aware of the competition, including the new competition (AI). You need to form deeper, stronger, and more value-based relationships with your existing clients. You need to

know them more, understand what they need, survey them, and interact with them monthly.
3. Are you a TRUSTED RESOURCE? This concept says anybody in my Sphere of Influence contacts me before a refinance, putting on a new roof, new sewer, new flooring, new landscaping, etc. The list goes on and on. Your goal should be to be the trusted resource, so your sphere will not consider doing anything to the home unless they contact you first because you are their trusted resource.
4. Are you a local CELEBRITY? A social celebrity? A sphere celebrity? Americans have no idea how attracted they are to celebrities. It is time for you to plan, strategize, and get in the media. In the following pages, there are some hints, but to be clear, if you want to increase your sales, you need to level up your celebrity game!
5. No one will value you if you do not value yourself. It is easy to know if a person has self-worth or not. Are you learning daily? Are you leading daily? How are you showing up? What is your energy level? What is your competence level? How are you dressing? How is your physical appearance? I can assure you this, as a 19-year-old broker, I was in a suit and tie every day, and I outsold them all. I had zero experience, but I always looked good and was mentally ready for opportunity, are you? Simply showing up and having the passion and energy to serve, solve, and create is the real value people want. Don't let them rule you out because you are casually dressed and casually groomed. People who want to be led in a transaction do not want a casual agent!

18

GIVE VALUE FIRST

*"When there's no **value**, all that's left is the **price**."*
—Jeffrey Gitomer

Value is defined simply as this: something done for the customer, on behalf of the customer, before the sale. That is value. What value do you bring to the marketplace? What are you doing for your customers before you make a sale? That's what you are going to focus on in this section. This section is going to inspire you and spark something in your mind that says, "I have to start delivering more value. I have to start giving before getting. I have to start doing things before the sale, so people are attracted to me and want to do business with me!"

I'm telling you this: Nobody trains on this stuff. I can only tell you that after over 30 years, thankfully, I've provided enough value in several different ways that my team and I have been able to sell 130 homes and gross close $720,000 in income. I can directly attribute most of that to what I've done for people *before* the sale. It's taken me over 30 years of building value. So, don't get frustrated; get fascinated. Try to take my 30 years and turn it into 5.

Be Different

How are you **different**? Come up with three reasons why you're different from everybody else. People want to know how you're different. Are you sending recipe cards or custom-made cards with great messages on them? Do you have a computer program that will allow you to customize and personalize your messages? What is it that makes you stand out from the hundreds of other agents in your area? Number one should be, "I ask better questions than anybody else in the marketplace."

Value can be found in...

- The **depth** of your questions
- Your knowledge or expertise
- Your brand
- Your involvement in your community

How am *I* different? I coached football for 25 years at a high school. We had approximately 80 children per season. 80 x 25 years is a hell of a lot of families that I touched. We won a lot. That helped grow my Sphere of Influence.

Do you know how many homes I sold because I was Coach Bill? I never received a dime for coaching for 25 years, but because I gave of myself, people said, "You're a good guy. You're going to be our real estate agent."

Understand that people do business with their friends. What are you doing in the community? What are you involved in your life that is bigger than yourself?

Mine happened to be coaching. Hopefully, for you, it's something that's a passion. When you look at that area of your life, you're going to get a lot of business from it. If you're not doing that, you need to find something that you care about that's bigger than yourself and start delivering. You don't do it to get the rewards, you do it because of who you become, but that will pay you. If you're doing nothing for anybody else, you're probably not going to get any business from it because you're no different from anybody else.

Why Do I (The Client) Need You?

When relaying your value to clients, remember these important reasons they need to work with you:

1. **I can get you the highest price.** Do you think you can get more for a home than a For Sale By Owner? You better believe it. There's no question. How do we get a seller more money for their home than a For Sale By Owner? The bottom line is who will drive more competition to the home? Who's linked in with people that sell homes? The answer to the question is: I bring more buyers and more exposure to your home. I can put a million eyes on your home from a national website.
2. **I am not emotionally involved.** A seller needs an unemotional third party. The only way you understand it or don't understand it is to see it happen in your career. Over 25 years, I've seen sellers and buyers without real estate agents mess their deals up. I've seen money left on the table. Either you know that you can negotiate a deal better for your buyer or seller, or you don't. If you're brand new, then you're going to have to figure it out. My guess is with this training, you're still going to be better simply because you're an unemotional third party. Real estate is the most emotional sale in the world. Probably wise to have an unemotional third party.
3. **I do this every day.** When people ask you, "Why do I need you?" you can tell them, "I'm selling

homes every day. Our company's selling homes every day. How many are you selling?" People upset me when they think they know how to sell homes better than me when they don't do it every day. And it should upset you. Don't sit there when I come into a listing, or with a buyer, and say that you know more than me, because you don't.

4. **Do you really have the time?** As a buyer or a seller, do you really have the time to do this yourself? One of my favorite things I like saying is, "How do you like being a real estate agent? Do you run criminal background checks before buyers come into your home? Do you mean your husband is not running a criminal background check on the buyers that come into your home? Oh my gosh! Wow, not good."

5. **I can get you the lowest price.** Can you get a buyer a lower price? If the buyer says, "Can you really get me a lower price?" You say, "Yes! I can get you a lower price." When buyers are wondering if they can purchase for less, I always say, "Tell me what you think you can buy it for. If I don't get you a lower price, I don't need to be paid." I always get them a lower price, but I make them really love the home first to try and get that value out of them.

6. **I do this every day. (Legal mistakes)** There are legal issues, right? Contracts are scary. When we want to scare a customer, we want to talk about the contracts and legal mistakes they may make. I'm not saying we're as good as an attorney, but I'm saying we do this every day and understand what goes on. Do buyers and sellers have any idea what they're signing when they sign a personal agreement or listing contract? No.

7. **I offer emotional support.** It's okay to talk to people about this. "Mr. and Mrs. Buyer/Seller, this is an extremely emotional time." Talk to them about the emotional angles of buying or selling. "I want to make sure you're not making decisions out of emotion, so I'm going to be there to help you understand the facts of what's going on." In the same breath, if they love the home, write the offer. Sometimes you need to encourage their emotion and say, "Hey, let's do it."

Ten Ways to Give Value First

1. **Give creative and out-of-the-box advice.** How do you become creative? First, study creativity. Look at top producers who are creative, people who think and act outside the box. Look at successful people and get more creative about how you approach listings and buyers.

I constantly come up with creative ideas. I was at a listing, $900,000 on the water, that was a teardown. The seller looked at me and said, "Glenn, you're telling me the value is in the lot? The house has no value?" I had to tell him, "The house has no value." Can you imagine saying that on a $900,000 home? Your home is worth nothing. I said, "Here's what I'm going to do. I'm going to invite every builder and every developer for a builder/developer wine and cheese party. They'll help you see where the real value is."

What can you do differently when you go to list a property? Ice cream and coffee open houses. Everybody's got the same old cookies and water bottles. Don't be afraid to spend a little money to be creative and outside the box.

Creative also can be in terms of financing. There are all types of creative ways to do financing. We talked about paying two years in taxes to decrease down payments. Rent-to-buy programs and assumptions are coming back into the market. Being creative and knowing how to talk about assumptions when you're selling a home is probably good to sell FHA because if rates go through the roof, you're going to have a marketable asset that is at 4%. That is when people will say, "Wow, no other real estate agent has told me that."

What tools are you giving your customers to use that have value? What are you doing to engage your clients? How are they getting engaged? Are you Tweeting your open houses? Are you posting your open houses on Facebook? Are you giving them real-time searches on where they live? Are you pointing them to websites that help them get information they don't have? Are you giving them information that helps them build equity in their property? Are you hiring networking groups to help them build their business, not just your business? Are you giving them value first before you ask for the sale? Or are you just taking referrals and sending them crappy gifts?

2. **Look, act, and be more professional and friendly than anybody else in the marketplace.** It is essential to be professional. I really believe in friendly service. People like friendly people. So please, be more friendly. Your SOS Challenge on this is: I'm

going to be more friendly to people. I'm going to be nicer to people.

3. **Speak at local clubs.** You want to become *the local* expert. Kiwanis Clubs, Rotary Clubs, REALTOR clubs, business clubs, networking groups, and chamber of commerce groups are always looking for speakers. Speaking is free, but you can make a lot of money speaking. Simply prepare a 10–15-minute value message for any of those clubs.

Call and say, "Hi, I'm a local REALTOR in the community. I'd like to give a 10–15-minute report at the Rotary Club on what's happening in real estate. I'd also like to include what I consider to be the three best values in our marketplace. Do you think you would be interested in that?" Groups are looking for speakers all the time. I encourage you to target local clubs and audiences and begin speaking and educating people on real estate. Then you become the expert.

4. **Write in local arenas: blogs, boards, and papers**. Write, write, write. Writing leads to tremendous wealth. Imagine if you started an awesome blog. I'm not saying this is for everybody, but you might be able to create The Secret to Real Estate blog or The Secrets of Buying and Selling blog. You're just throwing out lists of how to buy lower and how to sell higher. People start picking up on it, and you become the expert. Great way to build value. Creating content on Nextdoor, hyper-local websites, for local newspapers, bigger newspapers, business journals, and inserts for vendor mailouts are all free ways to get your name into the community!

5. **Post video testimonials on your website.** What video testimonials do you have, and are they on your website? It is one thing to tell a potential buyer and seller how good you are. It is quite a different thing to have a past buyer or seller tell your prospect how good you are. One of the best things we did was to have a party, hire a videographer who interviewed all my past clients, and post the videos on social media, Google, and my website. Video testimonials are powerful and very lucrative. Up your game and get those done!

6. **Lead a networking group that specifically benefits your best clients.** Networking groups are good. You can go to chamber events or start a networking group. This is a very easy, friendly way to become the expert.

7. **Occupational farming.** I don't know what career you were in before you got into real estate, but one of the best things I did was occupational farming. I farmed attorneys, specifically estate attorneys. Estate attorneys can give me listings easily. They have clients that die and have homes that need to be liquidated, and they don't care what the price is. I decided I was going to work with these people. So, I targeted ads in attorney's magazines. I had a list of service providers for attorneys, house trashes, clean-up people; I had a whole vendor list. The estate attorneys felt like I was making their job easy. I was doing something for them before asking for the listings. "I'll get your house cleaned out and cleaned up. I'll get your house painted. By the way, since I'm doing all this, would you mind giving me the listing?"

SOURCE OF SALES (SOS)

There are dentists, accountants, financial planners; you can target occupations and be of service to these people. Let's use retirement communities as an example. I made a ton of money buddying up to the people. Do you understand that old people walk into retirement communities, and they are told, "We're getting ready to take all of your net worth, so you need to sell your home"? How do you get in front of the people who can get you those listings? What does every retirement director need? Entertainment and education. If you can give the person sitting in a retirement community a little entertainment and a little education to help make their life easier, they will refer business to you.

You might set up a meeting and say, "I've invited ten people who have the same career as you to get together and network on how to become a more effective person who takes old people's monies from their homes. I'm going to show you a few business ideas. Would you be interested in coming? We're going to serve great food." Make that networking event happen, and they're all going to call you and say, "Mrs. Crabtree needs to sell her home because we need to take all of the equity in her home."

You'd be amazed at what you can do for apartment managers to help them. "Hey, I want to get you and ten other managers together and share best practices. I have ten great ways to help you reach 100% occupancy. Are you interested? I'll have great food. Come on, let's just network." After you feed them and give them great ideas, you say, "Would I be able to do a first-time homebuyer program in your apartment building?"

8. **Create a website that delivers secret information.** I told you I have home buying secrets. Everybody loves a secret. Everybody wants to have something they can't have. I love the idea of promoting home buying secrets. Imagine if you could post information that seems confidential, that's valuable that people would want to know. They would go to your site. I like things that say: "Lowest priced homes on the lake," "Lowest priced homes on the golf course," "Best foreclosures." The bottom line is you have to market it. Put yourself in front of people that can say yes.

9. **KNOW what others don't know.** Ask what others can't. Deliver where others fail. That's the essence of value. People are not delivering in our marketplace. It's time for us to start delivering.

10. **Have the guts to speak the truth.** That's a value. I've had so many people in this market tell me, "Glenn, you're the first agent who has really had the guts to tell me the truth." We get all fluffy and want to be liked, but sometimes people need a gutsy sales guy to say, "Hey, here's the reality on this deal." Especially if you're the second or third guy in on a listing, Boom! Hit them with it. If they've already failed, if it's an expired, say, "Here's the deal. Let's do this." Speak the truth, and they'll love it. It gives certainty.

Know Your Value

We're in one of the hardest industries that there is. You work very, very hard for your money. We can spend a ton of money in this business. I believe that we should be the highest paid people in the marketplace. If you do not know your value or

SOURCE OF SALES (SOS)

do not know how to communicate your value, you're giving money away. I met with a real estate agent, a commission cutter, who gave away $42,000 in fees a year. That's crazy. I believe that we should be paid better than anybody on Earth. The reason we don't is that we don't feel our value. What is your value in the marketplace? How do you communicate your value? Do people value you? Jeffrey Gitomer says, "When there is no value left, all that is left is price." If you go into listings and people are pounding you on your fee, the reason is you're not doing anything for the seller, on behalf of the seller, before asking him to sign a listing. Price is not the issue.

Ask what their three most important considerations are when deciding who to hire as their agent. If they answer, take note, and deliver on those three things. In fact, over-deliver on those three things.

Some people may just want the best deal. As an SOS professional, you should now know the proper responses on dealing with this reply.

"How would you define the best deal?" You can use their three most important considerations against them. Inherently, what they want most will not necessarily allow them to get the cheapest or best deal.

I have given you several things you can do to put yourself in front of buyers and give value. We talked about helping other people build their businesses. We talked about starting a website, bestgolfcoursehomes.com, bestvaluesinrealestate.com, and so on. I own broadripplehomes.com. I have a tab that says the lowest price per square foot listings. Click here to obtain this list. They click. Then, they have to register their email. Sorry, you're not going to get that information without me getting information on you.

19

BUILD TRUST

Trust is obviously extremely important. I want to talk to you a little bit about building trust. Here's when you don't have it. When sellers don't list at your price at full commission, they don't trust you. When buyers don't offer a reasonable price on a home, they don't trust you.

You are trusted when you say, "Here's what I think it will sell for," and they say, "List it." When you have a buyer, and they say, "What do you think we should offer?" You say, "Well, based on the information, I think you should be somewhere in this range," and they listen to you. If that's not happening, you don't have trust. If you don't have trust, try some of these ideas.

7 Ways to Build Trust

1. **Show up on time.** Be well prepared. Be well-groomed. Dress for success. I believe that perception is reality. If you look like a slob, they're going to think you're a sloppy real estate agent. Your first impression must be good. I don't think you can overdress for a

client. It pays to look good. It's unfair, but perception is perception.

2. **Be upbeat and personable without being overly personable or familiar.** You don't want to start hugging the person who walks through the open house door; however, you want to be upbeat and personable.

3. **Mirroring works (body language and speaking).** If you've got an excited client, be excited. If you've got a calm guy, be calm! Otherwise, they're going to go, "This guy is driving me crazy." I've lost deals because of that. My personality doesn't match up with most people, but I adjust my level of excitement to fit the client.

4. **What is the best way to listen?** Avoid the temptation to interrupt, critique, or argue. The best way to listen is to write down everything your prospect says. I have won many a listing because I simply wrote down everything my prospect said!

5. **Mention why you like working in real estate and with them.** Not to be cheesy, but to genuinely care for and be interested in your prospect is a huge value. Especially if you can parlay that into helping them, their friends, and their families, especially their kids!

6. **Marketing materials should be up-to-date, current, and accurate.** The materials should be about what the client wants, not about you. Personal brochures are gone. We all have websites and Facebook pages. I'm encouraging you to stop putting

things about yourself in your marketing materials. People don't care about you; they care about themselves and their needs. Look at what your marketing materials are saying. If it's focused on you, "I'm the greatest in the world, I sell a lot of homes, yadda-yadda-yadda," people become disinterested.

When you have marketing material, the marketing material should be geared towards the customer. When the customer reads it, they're going, "Wow, there's real value here. There's information that answers my questions. There's information in here that makes me say thank you to the person who gave it to me. There's information in this marketing piece that I actually appreciate and has real value."

Get rid of old cards and brochures. Update all your information. What agent tools do you have at your disposal, and are you using them? Please update your photo. Some photos are amusing. I'm like, "Who is this? Hi, I just did this deal with you, and you're not the same agent as the one on your card."

7. **Find common ground quickly, whether sports, local news, or family.** Notice what's hanging on the wall. When I go into a home, I always examine what is hanging on the wall. Usually, I could find something on the wall to talk about. If not, ask them about it and compliment them. Say, "Wow, that's interesting."

Your clients won't value you if they do not trust you. Do not skip this step. Building trust benefits both you and your client, and the entire process will go more smoothly.

20

BRANDING YOURSELF

*"Your customer wants to do
business with a somebody, not a nobody."*
—Jeffrey Gitomer

I'll tell you what else is value - your brand. Do you have a brand? Everyone does. The question is this: Is your brand what you want it to be? How are you perceived in the marketplace? What's your slogan? If you don't have a slogan, you don't have a brand. People want to do business with a somebody; they don't want to do business with a nobody. Google yourself and find out if you're somebody or nobody. Go to Facebook to find out if you're somebody or nobody. Go to Twitter to find out if you're somebody or nobody. Go to YouTube to find out if you're somebody or nobody.

I'm not saying that you're nobody, just that you're nobody in real estate. People want to do business with somebody they can find. They want to work with someone they can touch and feel and experience before calling you. If you don't think people are walking out of your open houses, opening their phone, and looking you up on Google or Facebook to see if you're legit, then you're wrong, because they are. It's happening.

Delusion #1: The public cares about your business.

Reality: The bottom line is the public doesn't know you exist if you're not branding. They don't care about your business because they don't know you exist.

Delusion #2: You believe you are offering something different and superior to your competitors. Reality: You're offering pretty much the same service when it comes down to listing and selling real estate. Your advice and your persuasion make the difference.

Here's my branding.

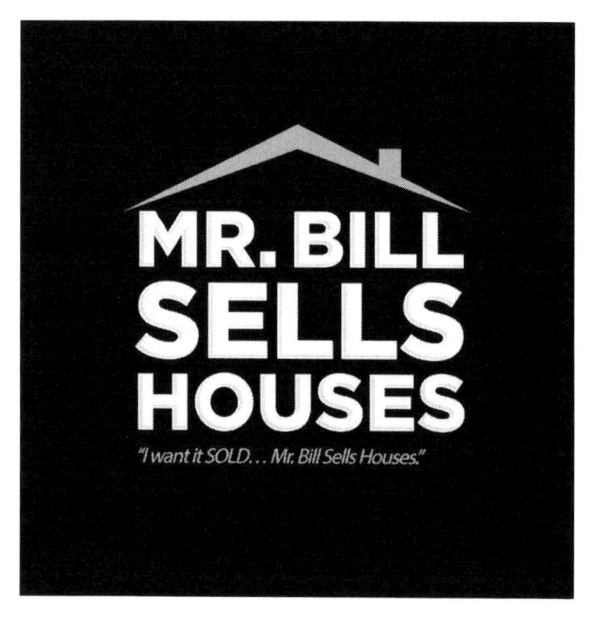

Mr. Bill sells houses.

SOURCE OF SALES (SOS)

Glenn Bill Group.

Here's my hyper-local branding, Broad Ripple Homes.

All very similar. People know I exist. I've been really working on a consistent brand to help me with what we're doing.

Google Me!
GLENN BILL

Look at the back of my business card. How about putting that on the back of your card? Especially if you're social media savvy. You put that on the back of your card, people are going to go, "Wow, that is a cool card." Then they are going to Google you. When they Google you, you're going to have your website set up. When they go there, they go, "Man! That dude is for real!"

Branding Does 3 Things:

1. It turns your name and persona into a distinct product with desirable qualities associated with it - a pull. It's what pulls people to you. When I say get a slogan, I mean it. Understand that people call me just because they can't forget my name; it's Mr. Bill. That gets me money. I had a woman call me from Florida one morning, and she said, "I have to sell a home; you're the only agent's name I could remember in the marketplace. Can you list my home?" Yeah, I can. That's what you're missing if you don't have a slogan.
2. It attracts a more elite, more profitable clientele. When you're branded, people who are in the know, high-income earners, are going to follow your

SOURCE OF SALES (SOS)

brand. You're going to attract more elite and profitable clientele than people who aren't branded.
3. It helps you retain more of those top-quality clients, even when business is slow for everybody else. Being branded in the community and having people know you makes it so that when business is slow, it doesn't slow down for you. You're the go-to person. When everyone is quitting and leaving real estate, your brand is still there. It's a magnet; it attracts business.

12 Ways to Brand Yourself:

1. **Get your name as a domain name.** You need to get your name in your domain name to start increasing your Google ranking, so you become somebody on the internet, not a nobody. Get your domain name done.

2. **Build your website.** You can build websites for nothing.

3. **Write down the qualities that make you unique.** What qualities really make you unique?

4. **Write down a description of your clientele.** Think about the past two to three years:
Who was my clientele?
Who have I sold homes to?
What are those people like?
When you look at your website, marketing materials, and slogan, it should all point to your clientele. These

are the people you should probably target. It's called smart branding and smart marketing.

5. **Create a slogan or logo.** Logos are huge. If you have both, then you're really into it. Get both. You're in SOS. It's a challenge. I'm challenging you to do it.

6. **Blog and social network.** Remember the Facebook friend who made me $8,800 because I kept liking her comments. How many comments do you like a day? How many people are you liking? How many friends are you making on social networks? Social networking doesn't work unless you like a few people every day. Get on Facebook, even if you don't like it, click like.

7. **Schedule appointments with your best customers.** This might be THE most important thing that you get from this chapter. Who is your best customer?

Who's your best referral source, and what have you done for them? I would schedule an appointment with your two or three best customers by the end of the year and ask them why they chose you. Why do they think you're good? What have you provided of value?

Get a testimonial from them, buy them a very nice meal, and appreciate who they are. Then use their answers to these questions to improve your branding.

8. **Find cheap and free advertising targeting your specific markets.** There is very affordable and free advertising that can happen, especially on websites and social media. The question is, can you find it?

SOURCE OF SALES (SOS)

You've got to chunk it. Maybe one week, you need to go out into your community and find cheap advertising. Maybe a church bulletin.

Here's how I'm known in my church. I sponsor everything. I sponsor the festivals and trivia nights. I sponsor everything I can. If I can sponsor anything for $100, I'm sponsoring it. That's my litmus test. Anybody asks me for $100, I do it. I do it too much probably, but I make a lot of money; it's been good for me.

9. **Attend networking events.** I recommend Jeffrey Gitomer's *Little Black Book of Connections*. This is an awesome book on networking. I mean phenomenal. You could make $100,000 just networking if you read this book. It's one of the best books on networking and connections you can get. It's incredible.

10. **Redesign and improve yourself.** You're doing that by reading this book. You're redesigning and improving yourself – congratulations! Assess your life and your career goals. You should be thoughtfully answering this question, "What are my goals for branding?"

There are tools at your disposal that you are not using. Why aren't you using them? Because it's easy not to use them. "Hey, I'm selling 20 deals a year. It's cool. I don't need to grow." That may seem fine, but you're reading this for a reason. I think you want to grow. You want to become more of a winner in your eyes. You want to do more. I would encourage you to look at the tools that are available to you and grab one or two of them that you're not using and make it happen.

11. **Create a budget.** I don't know how much you want to spend. My guess is you do not have a budget for branding yourself. You might be thinking, "I don't want to create a budget. I don't want to commit to that."

What if you just committed $500 a month to branding? I mean, think about it. Six grand a year. If you're not getting any closings, it might be because you're not branded. It's like, what came first, the chicken or the egg? What came first, branding myself or a commission check?

12. **Find somebody that wants to sell and get a listing sign.** In the next 30 days, find somebody who wants to sell their home, list their property. and get it sold. That's the essence of real estate. You get to put your name on a sign. That will brand you. You can also put your slogan on the sign if you have a slogan. I recommend listings on high-traffic streets. Find the busiest street you can find and start listing property. Start directly targeting the busiest streets in your market. Then have your signs out there. That's the best way to do it.

Your Brand Characteristics

Define your brand with characteristics. What are your characteristics? I'm a great listener. I work hard. I return your text in five minutes or less. What are your characteristics? Think about who you've sold homes to in the past 2-3 years. What are those people like? What did they like about you?

Five Truths About Branding

1. It takes time. You're not going to finish reading this section and be a branding expert.
2. It grows organically. You can't necessarily force the growth.
3. It is not rational. Certain things can happen in branding where you just take off.
4. It demands absolute commitment. Either you're committed to your slogan and your logo and your branding, or you're not. If you're not committing to it, don't get into branding yourself because it won't work. Be committed with a budget and with time.
5. It always has an effect.

By now, you should be questioning your business model. I want you to look at what your most successful competitors are doing. Look around your market, find the successful people with branding, and copy them. There's a lot to be said for modeling. There's a lot to be learned by people who know how to brand themselves.

What tools do your customers have at their disposal? How **are you** helping them get/stay engaged? How do you ensure **you** are the **preferred choice**? Below are a few ways to start.

1. Think like your customers.
2. Ask and interview them.
3. Deliver what they need.
4. Treat them like family throughout the process.

21

21 WAYS TO BEAT THE COMMISSION OBJECTION

We must understand that the commission issue is usually within us, not with the customer. It's our inability to handle the objection. It's our inability to truly grasp that most commission objections can be handled within a minute. Most people want us to cut one point, if not more. On a $200,000 sale, that's two grand. That's $2,000 that you lose in one minute.

Five years ago, I met with one of our top producers. He felt very good about his production, but he was cutting commission. He realized he'd lost $47,800. Gone, off the table. He wasn't deliberately doing it; in fact, he was subconsciously doing it. He just didn't feel his value. It was easier to get signatures when he went along with the prospect on commission. At that moment, I realized I could equip REALTORS with 21 great responses when sellers ask us to cut commission.

If somebody is going to challenge you on commission, who's more uncomfortable, you or the seller? I believe the seller is. Have you ever asked somebody to reduce their fee? Does anybody take joy in screwing people out of what they earn? Would you be nervous if you asked your doctor or attorney to cut his fee? I want you to understand that when people ask you to cut your fee, they're nervous. They want that minute to go by just as quickly as you do; we think we're nervous, but they're more nervous. Understand the negotiation. This is why you are reading SOS today. These strategies are going to make you money.

I want to make some assumptions when we talk about charging full fees. Your presentations are professional, thorough, detailed, and visual. You can't charge high fees if you're not professional, if you're not thorough, if you're not detailed, and it's not visual. Those four things must exist, or you're going to have a tough time justifying your fee. You can't go in and justify your fee when you have terrible information. You need to have a persona of being a professional. If you go in and say, "I'm part-time, and I have a limited marketing plan," you're probably not going to charge a high fee.

My clients are all in a must-sell situation. We're face-to-face with the seller. I don't negotiate fees over texts or email. We're going to sit face-to-face. It's going to be a listing presentation, and it's going to be an instance where the seller needs to sell. I work with *have-to* clients. If you don't have to sell or buy, I don't have to work with you. That's number one. This must happen. This is a candidate, who, after my presentation, likes me, and wants to do business with me.

How do you know if they like you? Answer: You like them! Now, how do you feel about taking money out of the pocket of somebody you like? Not good! If they really like me, they don't ever ask me to take money out of my pocket. Being friendly and likable are very valuable commodities in this business. Are people doing business with you for you, or are they doing it because of your commission?

Why do people cut their fees? Answer: They want the listing! I understand you want the listing. Cutting your fee has nothing to do with you wanting the listing. You want to list it at a full fee and become more profitable in your business.

SOURCE OF SALES (SOS)

I'm in retail real estate, I charge more fees, and I'm prouder than anybody. You have to start becoming that way. You deserve it. This is not an easy business. I believe in you. Now, you need to believe in yourself as much as I do! I value you, and you need to value yourself and your time as much as I do! You need to be paid well.

21 Ways to Beat the Commission Objection

1. "No!" That's easy. They're going, "Oh, I feel uncomfortable, he said no. I didn't expect that."

2. Laugh and say, "No!" You can laugh first and then say no, or you can say no first and then laugh. Both work.

3. "Gosh, you know what, Mr. and Mrs. Seller, are any of the other agents negotiating their fee? The way that other agents negotiate their fee is very similar to how they're going to negotiate your price. For me to get you the highest and best value for your home, I don't think it's justifiable for me to cut my fee."

4. "Mr. and Mrs. Seller, I want you to ask the other agents if they have other properties listed at full commission. The other agents you're talking to, who are cutting the fee, do they have other properties at full fees? If they have other people paying them more, what level of service will you get? Simply put, if the other agent I'm competing against has a listing at six percent, and then they're going to list you at five percent, doesn't it make sense that you're going to get poor service from them? Mr. and Mrs. Seller, how would you feel if somebody paid you less, and other

people were paying you more? What type of service would you provide? If they're cutting for you and not cutting for others, that's a problem."

5. "I'm fortunate to have clients who feel I'm worth a full fee. I have ten other listings at that rate. I don't feel I could give you the service you deserve if you paid less. Doesn't that make sense to you? My fees are what they are. My fee is -X%. That's what I charge. I can't do you for less because if I do, I'm not going to treat you the same. I think you want to be treated the same."

6. "I'm curious. What's your profession? I'm just wondering, how would you feel if somebody came in and asked you to cut your fee 30%? My fee is 7%. If I co-op at 3.5%, I take 2 and a half. When they cut a point from me, it comes out of my pocket. That's a 29.5% reduction in my fee." They'd go, "Oh, God! I didn't even realize." Sometimes we have to walk through what that one point really means. It's not just one point; it's 30%.

7. "If we pay a co-op of a lower rate, I'm concerned other agents will not show your listing with full enthusiasm. Here's where I'm concerned, I'm known as a person who co-ops with other agents at the highest rate. Once I start cutting that down, the enthusiasm to show the home could be compromised. I don't want to take that chance. Let's go ahead and list it at a full fee." If I'm a buyer's agent, what homes do I like to sell the most? Of course, we want to sell the homes that our buyers love. What makes the deal even more fun for us as salespeople? Real estate agents who pay a significant frigging co-op fee.

SOURCE OF SALES (SOS)

8. "Do you not feel I'm worth it? Let's revisit my listing presentation so that I can justify my fee. I must've missed something in the presentation. Do you have an extra two hours so I can tell you?"

9. "Is commission more important than the agent you choose? What's the more important issue? Commission, the agent, or the service?" They can say yes, and you're done. Then you say, "That's fine. If it is, you know what, I'm not the agent for you. Go find somebody willing to work for nothing." If they say no, it's not the most important thing, then what are we really talking about? They're uncomfortable.

10. "After listening and considering my marketing presentation, do you feel like I'm the best agent you've interviewed? Mr. and Mrs. Seller, I know you've had 2 or 3 people in here. I know you're asking me to cut my fee, but the bottom line is, do you feel I'm the best or not?" Most people don't have the nerve to say, "No, you're not the best." "Well, if I'm not the best, you're not going to use me anyway, so obviously, I'm sitting here because I am the best." If they're asking you to cut your fee, aren't they telling you that you are the best? They want to do business with you. If they think you suck and really want to list with somebody else, they're not going to ask you to cut your fee; they're going to go, "Okay, well, that was a great listing presentation. We'll give you a call in the morning." If they're asking you to cut your fee, they're going, "I like this agent. Now, if I could just get a little extra sugar off the commission, I'll really like this agent." If they're asking you, they want to do business with you. That's the point.

11. "I feel like you feel like I'm the best choice for you. How much do you think an agent of lesser quality will cost you? Have you ever heard, 'You get what you pay for?' Can an agent of lesser quality, who is not involved, not getting you exposure, not getting the extra fees, cost you? Think of all the things they could cost you because they're not diligent."

12. I love open houses and talking about open houses on listing presentations. I always like to say, "Mr. and Mrs. Seller, is the other agent who's cutting their fee willing to do an open house for the next four Sundays on your property?" No would be the answer. Here's the deal. If they get it based on price, and they have to do an open house every Sunday, won't it piss that discounting agent off? Every Sunday, you're going by, "Haha! You're not getting paid, and you're working every Sunday. Great Colts game!" I believe open houses can drive the price up at least 1%.

Here is a great example: Thursday, the buyer walks through and loves it. They schedule the second appointment for mommy and daddy to come through on Saturday. On Saturday, I have balloons and signs everywhere. The offer's written on Friday. We're negotiating, and I say, "Here's the deal; they want to do the open house. Let's call it, you can buy it for 154, and we don't have to do the open house, or we can do the open house, then, we'll continue to counter." I've gotten a higher price most of the time because the buyer says, "Don't hold the open house." "Mr. and Mrs. Seller, I'm willing to do that because this is about giving you the highest and best price. I will hold this home open. If I want the listing, I know it's good. What's the first point? It's going to sell in the first week anyway. I'm not going to have to hold it open for four Sundays. Especially if I price it right. Demonstrate how that one open house technique can get you an extra point on your sale. The other agent won't do that.

13. Use the Objection Handling Track. "You don't want to pay a full fee? Great." You're going to feed it back. You're going to hear it out. You're going to question it. "You're the seller! Why don't you want to pay a full fee?"
"It's going to mean more money that I have to bring to the table."
"Well, let me ask you this question. Based on the marketing information, and based on all the exposure I can give you, and because I'm willing to hold four straight open houses, and based on the fact that I have a complete marketing program that's unbelievable, don't you think that I can get you the highest possible price for your home, based on my competition?" They may say, "No, I think everybody does the exact same thing."
"Great, so, you think everybody does the exact same thing?" Go ahead and feed it back again. Question the importance. "How important do you think it is that you have an agent that does more or does less? How important is it that you get the most eyes on your property? How important is it for you to get the most for your home? I know that you'll have to continue to put more money out at closing, but if you hold this home for three to four months, how much money is that going to cost you? If it costs you that much more, are you really spending less by going with the lesser agent at a lesser fee?"

14. Calculate what you're really making based on a 120-day transaction. Now, they don't care about what you really make on a 120-day transaction. This is what I call the sympathy close on commission. "Mr. and Mrs. Seller, I want you to understand, I may be with you for the next 120 days. If we really look at the fee that I'm charging you of $6,000, by the time I split it with my broker, it's $3,000. By the time they raise the income tax, that will take 30% of my income, so I'm really doing this for $2,000. When I look at the hard expenses that it takes to market your property, that's easily going to be another $500, so you're asking me to work for you for three months for $1,500. Do you think that's a pretty good deal?"

Walk through it with them. Make them feel like they're getting an absolute steal with the full fee. There are expenses involved. What's the great thing about listing? If you list it right, and you list it below market, it's not going to take 120 days, but you don't tell them that. We can get it sold, boom, now. The point is there are costs involved with marketing real estate. You need to know what they are, which will help you have more resolve when it comes to justifying your fee.

15. "I would cut my fee for you, but my sales manager won't let me. Now, if you want to call Susan and talk to her, I'm sure she would be more than happy to talk to you about why we are worth it."

16. Talk about net proceeds. In the section on **Seller Mastery**, I gave you 21 reasons why you want to use that net proceeds form. That net proceeds form is a great tool. Sellers don't have a chance with you if you go back to the net proceeds. Sellers who are making

SOURCE OF SALES (SOS)

money, or are receiving funds in excess of your commission, need to focus on the net. Everybody loves cash. Everybody loves certainty.

17. "Do you feel my service is superior to my competitors? If so, you're asking me to charge less for superior service. Do I bring more to the table in terms of value than my competitors? I'd like to ask you, have you ever flown first class? Did it cost you more upfront? There's a reason. I can't give you first-class service for a second-class price." It's called the airplane close.

18. "You know what? I'll consider cutting my fee. When you ask me to cut my fee 1%, that represents a 29.5% reduction in my professional service fee. I'll make you a deal. You reduce your price 29.5%, and I'll reduce my commission 29.5%." That's a good one. They hate that one. We're in this together. We're a team. You wouldn't ask your teammate to do that.

19. "I'm very fortunate that I have been referred to you by your friends, the Smiths. As you know, I've sold 3 or 4 different homes for the Smiths, and they've paid me a full fee every time. The only thing I'd want to know is how would the Smiths feel if I cut the fee for you and not for them? What do you think? It wouldn't feel too good. Out of respect for them and for you, I think we should keep it at a full fee and move down the road. You understand?"

People get very upset when they refer you to people, and you do a different fee for them. They're the people that referred you. Hello! No more referrals for you. He did it for what? Do you not think, if they beat you on the commission, they're actually going to call their friends, the guy did it for 2% less than you got it." That ends a relationship.

20. "How will your friends feel if you got my business for less than them? How would you feel if you referred me, and I did business less for your friends? I don't want you to feel that way, so we're going to go ahead and do it at a high fee." I realize this is much the same as the technique above, but it is a shorter and more direct way to go about it.

21. **Now is the time for you to write your own commission objection handling technique and send it to me at glenn@glennbill.com. I may even post it in our SOS Facebook group!**

Value Mastery: SOS Challenge

Start bringing Value Mastery to your business by completing the exercises in the *SOS Playbook*. If you don't already have your *SOS Playbook*, visit www.glennbill.com/sosplaybook to download your copy.

CONCLUSION

My friend in real estate,

I hope you enjoyed the book and have discovered who you are and why you are in this fantastic business of real estate. Most importantly, I hope you found out what and who your Source of Sales are.

You cannot succeed and be a leader in this business unless you can answer the two questions: who am I, and what am I all about? Once you have figured that out, mastering all the secrets of real estate success becomes easy and perfected through your repetition of the content in this book.

From reading SOS, you learned lessons from many of the great real estate agents who came before us. We all owe them a debt of gratitude. However, SOS is more than just a collection of sales techniques; it is a revolution in sales and is the next wave to ride to your success. This is the Source for your happiness, freedom, creation, wealth, and, most importantly, SALES!

While reading this book, I hope you took the time to complete the exercises in the *SOS Playbook* to deepen your understanding of the Five Pillars of Mastery. If you have not yet taken the time to enhance your understanding of you own

Conclusion

Source of Sales, take the time now to visit www.glennbill.com/sosplaybook to access your copy of the *SOS Playbook*.

I've been in real estate for over 30 years, and the most important thing I've discovered is that learning directly from a mentor is the quickest way to reach your goals. Just as any top professional athlete has a coach to help them achieve success, so should you. If you want to go deeper into the SOS process, then I invite you to attend an SOS event with me and my team. Learn more at www.getsosevent.com.

RECOMMENDED READING

Little Red Book of Selling: 12.5 Principles of Sales Greatness: 12.5 Principles of Sales Greatness: How to Make Sales Forever by Jeffrey Gitomer

Little Black Book of Connections: 6.5 Assets for Networking Your Way to Rich Relationships by Jeffrey Gitomer

Customer Satisfaction is Worthless, Customer Loyalty is Priceless: How to Make Customers Love You, Keep Them Coming Back and Tell Everyone They Know by Jeffrey Gitomer

How to Master the Art of Selling by Tom Hopkins

Mastering the Art of Selling Real Estate by Tom Hopkins

Mastering the Art of Selling Real Estate by Tom Hopkins

The Official Guide to Success by Tom Hopkins

ABC's of Attitude: Discover Your Secret Formula to Achieve Success in Your Personal and Business Life, Increase Your Emotional Intelligence and GET ATTITUDE! By Glenn Bill

ACKNOWLEDGMENTS

I would like to thank the following people who have supported me, moved me forward, challenged me, and always encouraged me to Get Better, Glow Brighter, Grow Bigger, and Go Beyond.

First, as mentioned in the book, was the man who initially spotted my talent at 18 years old, Mr. Dusty Asbury. Thank you also to Carl Van Rooy, who gave me my first job in Real Estate.

I want to also thank my first broker, Mr. David Harling, who was the only one who would hire a broke nineteen-year-old who had a full-time college schedule and a third shift job.

I'd also like to thank Mr. Neil Lantz (AHM Graves) and Dave Wilcox (FC Tucker) who chose to pass on the longshot kid with a big dream and an unending drive to succeed. Many successful people have worthy adversaries whom they need to prove wrong. Both these men were great leaders in the industry and playfully watched me dominate the market as I grew!

Even though I did not go to work for him either, I need to thank Mr. Jim Litten of the FC Tucker Company who served as a mentor and guide to me as I was building our company. I literally said in many meetings as industry semantics were brought up, "Let's just do whatever FC Tucker and Jim are doing." That proved to be a great compass and decision.

Next is Mr. Earl Owen, who was on floor call during my first week. Man, do we have stories! He has passed, but he taught me so much about never taking no for an answer and that there is "no debtors prison" for the hundreds of deals he had me write. I thank you for your friendship and memories I will never forget.

Perhaps the biggest shift in my career was when Mr. Steve Decatur and Tim O'Connor made me a partner in a little company (CENTURY 21 at the Crossing, In the Village, and On the Avenue) that we grew together into a three-office firm. We competed against the best, created a culture that will never be matched, and achieved heights that most of our competitors thought were unimaginable.

To all the agents and staff whom we grew with as an ownership group, I thank you. My most fond memories in real estate were during those years. Some of my best friends, mentors, and inspirations come from my relationships with you…too many to list, but you know who you are!

Source of Sales was born after we SOLD our little diamond in the rough to Mr. Mick Scheetz and Tracy Hutton. I'd like to thank each of them for setting me free to engage in my passion of training, motivating, and inspiring the agents of CENTURY 21 Scheetz!

I must especially thank Ms. Patty Bender, who introduced me to another mentor, Mr. Jeffrey Gitomer, but most importantly, tirelessly produced my power points in the beginning.

Mr. Jason Cline in our graphics department came up with the original logo and graphics; his work was followed up by Blake Daniels, and last but not least, Corina Splendoria designed the layout of the workbook.

To all the agents who have thanked me, done testimonials, and joined our @sourceofsales Facebook group, I thank you!

To all the agents in MIBOR whom I had cross-sales with, I thank you, especially all those agents who were in the Glenn Bill Group at one time or another, including Steffanie

Salzmann who has never left; you are a great friend and confidant.

To all my assistants, especially Mrs. Diane Wyant and my personal MVP Mrs. Kelly Glogoza. Perhaps no other person in my professional life has done more for myself, our buyers and sellers, and all our agents and co-op agents than Kelly. She is beloved by all who come in contact with her, and she is often given credit for my success; I must say I cannot argue with that!

I'd like to thank my team who helped finish this ten-year book project, Carly and Rory Carruthers, and Riley Molinaro.

Lastly, I'd like to thank all the mortgage lenders and real estate offices across the nation who have hired me to come speak in their towns so their most important people can find their Source of Sales.

ABOUT THE AUTHOR

Glenn Bill is the Creator and Founder of the Source of Sales System: America's #1 How-To Real Estate Sales Training Program. He is also the #1 International Best Selling Author of *The ABC's of ATTITUDE* and *Source of Sales (SOS)*. Additionally, he is the Founder of the University of Attitude, Global Attitude Awareness Day, and The Attitude Movement.

Glenn has been in the real estate business since 1988 as an accomplished REALTOR, Team Leader, and Broker/Owner. He also sits on the Board of Directors of his local Board of REALTORS®. He has been recognized annually as being in the Top 1% in sales for an International Sales organization with over 130,000 sales associates.

Glenn Bill also hosts the National Award-Winning Podcast: The Get Attitude Podcast (the GAP). Some of the most iconic, legendary, and successful people in the real estate industry, mortgage industry, and personal development industry have shared their trade secrets, heartfelt personal stories, and journeys. Guests share how they bridged the GAP from who they were to who they wanted to become.

Glenn, a 13-year member of the National Speakers Association, travels the world giving keynote addresses to all industries regarding attitude related to sales, customer service, disruption, leadership, diversity/inclusion, and personal and business success. His keynote speeches cover increased production, profitability, and morale for their team or company. His mission is to change the world "one attitude at a time."

However, his most important accomplishment and greatest source of inspiration for his attitude and passion is the fulfilling life he has created with his childhood sweetheart and their four children. They are the WHY behind his drive, success, and fulfillment.

NOTES

2. Rules of Self Mastery

1. trademark by Gitomer, Jeffrey H.
2. Ajin. "Understanding Our Mind - Ajin." Medium, 25 July 2020, https://medium.com/@ajingeorge96/understanding-our-mind-1168f442b36. Accessed 12 Feb. 2022.

8. Engagement Questions

1. Hopkins, Tom. *How to Master the Art of Selling.* Grand Central Publishing, 2005.

12. Seller Objections

1. Hopkins, Tom. *How to Master the Art of Selling.* Business Plus, 2005.

Made in the USA
Columbia, SC
18 February 2023